WHO *KNOWS*

WHO *KNOWS* WINS

Using Information to Create and Sustain Strategic Advantage

Ketan J. Patel
Partner, KPMG

JORDANS
1996

Published by
Jordan Publishing Limited
21 St Thomas Street
Bristol BS1 6JS

British Library Cataloguing-in-Publication Data
A catalogue record for this book is available from the British Library.

ISBN 0 85308 209X

Typeset by Mendip Communications Limited, Frome, Somerset
Printed by Hobbs the Printers of Southampton

ACKNOWLEDGEMENTS

Special thanks to Papa. The help of Nada Spendall, Mark McDonnell and James Clavell made this book possible.

CONTENTS

INTRODUCTION

'O divine art of subtlety and secrecy! Through you we learn to be invisible, through you inaudible and hence we can hold the enemy's fate in our hands.'

Sun Tzu, *The Art of War*, fifth century BC

Who Knows Wins explores the essence of information and how it is used by strategists, tacticians and their advisers to win in competitive situations. The book looks at the guidance of some of the great ancient strategists (Sun Tzu, Miyamoto Musashi and Alexander the Great) and strategic thinkers and analysts of our time (Michael Porter, Philip Kotler and Charles Handy), and the lessons to be learnt from some of the current winning corporate strategies (General Electric, Hewlett Packard and Dell Computers). The book also provides a number of frameworks to enable the reader to take positive action for better utilising intelligence.

Through an unconventional look at the whole area of information and knowledge, *Who Knows Wins* provides a practical guide on how to use information to lead an organisation through strategic, tactical and transformational change.

The book addresses itself to the key questions facing the chief executive officer in managing and leading change in a competitive environment:

- How do you determine the basis of **power and influence** in the organisation?
- What information do you need not only to benefit from **macro-level changes** but to influence the changes themselves?
- What should you know about **yourself and your rivals** to determine the best position for yourself?

- How do you decide how you can best **attack, defend or retaliate** in any given situation?
- How can **tactics** be used to gain advantage?
- In light of the above, how should you develop a programme to **lead your organisation** through transformational change?

Chapter One explores the themes of information and knowledge, which play a critical part in the exercise of power and influence. Without them a business cannot achieve its ends.

The environment and its relationship with companies are explored in Chapter Two. Knowledge of the macro-level environment enables a business to understand the forces that may buffet it and knock it off course. While some have spectacularly and opportunistically used the macro-changes to their advantage, others have changed the course of the macro-forces themselves, ie stock markets, governments and regulatory bodies.

Chapter Three shows how an organisation's knowledge of itself, its rivals and its position is critical to determining its response to the forces playing upon it.

Chapter Four investigates the information required to succeed in the strategy and tactics of attack, defence and retaliation, with the help of Sun Tzu and Michael Porter. The outcomes of the annual planning and budgeting round are rarely as imagined and the importance of creating and seizing opportunities is recognised as a key to success.

The need to respond to the world around us is continued in Chapter Five in an examination of the information required for tactical manoeuvring.

Chapter Six enters the world of the boardroom to help create an agenda for leading an organisation. The previous chapters are drawn together in a structured way to demon-strate how knowledge of the environment, the organisation, its rivals and position should be used to create purpose, determine the change agenda, and monitor and fuel change.

The Appendix to the book provides two simple illustrations of the very basic analysis required to examine the position of an organisation within its industry.

The leader is the key to the success of the business. Each chapter of this book will consider one of six fundamental leadership challenges:

- understand the role of power and influence in winning
- decide how to benefit from and become the architect of macro-change
- develop insight into the capabilities and flaws of your organisation, your rivals and your competitive battlegrounds
- ensure you pick fights that you can win and win the fights that you pick
- manoeuvre your rivals not just your own organisation
- draw up an agenda to lead your organisation to victory now and to get to the future first.

The key leadership qualities and attributes needed to meet these challenges are considered, as well as the responsibilities you must discharge to be worthy of the position of leader. Each chapter shows how the consummate leader is a strong and extreme mix of the four dimensions illustrated in Figure i below, possessing:

- a deep sense of belief and destiny that guides judgements and actions
- efficient mental processes that provide extreme clarity, speed, breadth and learning
- far-reaching visualisation, enabling the future possibilities to be imagined
- relationship skills that allow complex games to be played out and expectations to be shaped.

Figure i   *Key leadership qualities*

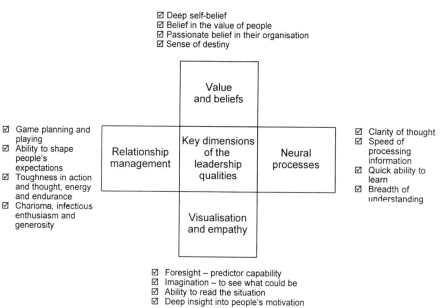

Frameworks, techniques and case studies may be useful aids, but it is the qualities listed above that are essential to meet the challenges of leadership.

The commitment to create the means – people, organisation, processes, systems, values and culture – to deliver the agenda laid out in this book is a significant undertaking. In determining whether the investment is worth making, the business has to ask itself if it can afford not to know; whether it is willing to make decisions to invest millions of pounds, dollars or roubles in ignorance of the relevant facts; and whether it will survive in ignorance of what its rivals, governments, suppliers and customers are doing and are about to do.

LEADERSHIP CHALLENGE
ONE

Understand the role of power and influence in winning

Alexander the Great wearing the diadem and horn of Zeus Ammon. The idealised features suggest his divinity.

Chapter One

KNOWLEDGE, POWER AND INFLUENCE

'In the beginning there was the Word. The Word was with God. The Word was God.'

The Gospel According to John

INTRODUCTION

We have all at some time in our lives been fascinated, enraptured and possessed by knowledge, almost as if this would reveal the mysteries of the universe, make us better able to handle the world around us, even make us more powerful. The idea is also planted at the back of our minds that knowledge is akin to godliness.

Strategy is the result of assimilating information, processing this against our accumulated knowledge bank, and planning the utilisation of resources and how to move and position them to achieve our goals.

The master strategist is that unique person who is better able to assimilate knowledge than his opponents and thereby forms superior strategies. Given our early fascination with knowledge, we can begin to understand the hero-worship that has existed around the strategist, this 'natural born' assimilator of knowledge and manipulator of information and people.

In this chapter, some of the key themes of knowledge, information, power and influence and the relationship between them will be explored. The ground covered is of vital importance to creating and sustaining winning strategies. We will begin by taking a look at the role that you, the leader, must play to meet the challenge. A brief account of the life of Alexander the Great provides an example of one of history's ultimate leaders.

MEETING CHALLENGE ONE

To meet the leadership challenge you must learn who has and will have power and influence in your organisation and in that of allies, rivals and stakeholders. You must learn how your power and theirs can shape the various outcomes that affect success and failure. The key leadership quality to meet this challenge is **visualisation and empathy**, which requires:

- the foresight to predict what such power could do
- the ability to see the web spun by the powerful and the influential
- a deep insight into people's motivation to determine why they choose to play the games they do.

This needs to be backed up by the **neural processes** that provide the clarity and the speed of thought to understand a moving power game.

Leadership entails significant responsibilities. These include ensuring that:

- the people with power and influence are understood
- the organisation appreciates the vital importance of intelligence to feed this understanding
- strategy and planning frameworks are available to utilise this intelligence.

If you cannot discharge this responsibility you will not be able to lead your organisation successfully, and others with less imagination and capability but more power will prevail.

ALEXANDER THE GREAT (356–323 BC)

Alexander the Great was embued with an excess of all the dimensions of leadership. His father, Philip the Great, had trained him in kingship, and for tutorship had secured the great philosopher Aristotle. Alexander led the Macedonian army at the age of 16, and at 20 he came to the throne. When Philip was assassinated, Alexander led a ruthless campaign to secure his home base, the Greek states and the mountain tribes. He had Thebes levelled and its 30,000 survivors sold into slavery; the other cities surrendered in fear. Then in 334 BC Alexander led the Macedonian army into Asia Minor where he defeated the Persian army and fleet, took control of the capital and pursued King Darius of Persia.

Alexander continued conquering the cities in his path. The fall of Gaza opened the way through marsh and desert to Egypt. Aged only 24, Alexander was welcomed enthusiastically and crowned as Pharaoh; he was regarded and worshipped as a living god by his Egyptian subjects. In one of the strangest episodes of his life, Alexander travelled through an eerie stretch of desert to visit the oracle of the ram-headed god Ammon at the oasis of Siwah on the remote western borders of Egypt and Libya. He was guided by two crows to reach the destination. On this visit, the purpose of which was said to be to 'learn of himself', Alexander was proclaimed the son of Zeus, which fitted well with his wish to see himself as a Homeric hero. Alexander finally overtook the fleeing Darius to find him murdered by his own men. He gave the king a proper royal burial and began the job of winning over the loyalty of the Persian nobility.

In 327 BC Alexander led his army through the wild mountain country of the Hindu Kush to India. The army crossed the River Indus in the north to meet fierce resistance. Alexander prevailed and marched on. He continued building monuments to the gods, poetry and festivity, and for philosophy an Indian holy man, a *sadhu*, joined him. As they marched eastward, Alexander's men believed they

would soon come upon the mythical river that they
believed surrounded the world. The troops had endured
the heat, hostilities and dangers of the Kush, sandstorms
and near starvation. They had followed their leader to the
ends of the earth. On the banks of the River Hydaspes,
Alexander could convince them to go no further. Legend
says that Alexander wept for there were no more lands to
conquer. He turned and led his army back home.

Alexander died at 32. His empire covered most of the
known world from the Danube and Adriatic South through
Greece, and from Egypt across Palestine into Turkey and
Iran and most of Afghanistan, Pakistan, the southern
provinces of Russia and Northern India. Alexander had
great visions of a kingdom in which all races were equal. He
led his troops in person regardless of personal danger.
There was nothing that he asked them to do that he would
not do himself. He was generous, solicitous, openhanded
yet firm in matters of discipline. He was also a cultured and
profound thinker and dreamer. Alexander's campaigns
covered every type of warfare and he was victorious in all
of them. He was totally aggressive in attacks, a master
practitioner of the first strike and innovative in his methods,
and he moved his army with a swiftness that caught his
enemies by surprise. A broad-thinking strategist he also
understood the importance of logistics and communications. Alexander secured his bases behind him,
replaced the worn-out veterans with new recruits and sent
supplies forward. His victories were based on careful
consideration of his potential enemies, their situations,
resources and the terrain. Alexander was happy to learn
from his enemies: he used the Persians' courier service and
used conquered local governments to collect taxes and
maintain towns. He was capable of winning by diplomacy,
fear or by beating his opposition into submission.
Worshipped as a mighty king and a god, Alexander was a
multi-talented strategist who others in history would be
hard pressed to equal.

USE OF INFORMATION

The ability to exercise power and influence the outcomes of corporate endeavour is a basic prerequisite for effective leadership.

A survey commissioned by KPMG and carried out by the Harris Research Centre encompassed 150 companies selected from the *Times 1000 Index*, excluding the top 200. Interviews were carried out with the relevant executive officer responsible for strategic planning – most commonly the managing, finance or strategic planning director. The results indicated that:

- between 53 and 81% of respondents made 'a lot' of use of internal information regarding their past financial performance, human resources, product profitability and cost structure
- 44% of companies use 'little or no' competitor information
- as much as 71 to 84% of companies used little or no macro-economic information.

The companies surveyed collected little information of use and what they did collect was little used! The survey confirmed that companies made regular and frequent efforts to know themselves but little effort to know their rivals and the impact of the external environment. In addition, a significant minority also received inadequate internal information to support their decisions and believed that their organisation's ability to analyse this information was poor.

The detailed results are given in Table 1 below.

Table 1 *Results of KPMG/Harris survey*

Information	Key findings	Implications
Performance monitoring	• 96% used performance indicators. • Only 47% set targets for performance based on their sector performance. • Only 41% compared their performance to key competitors. • 23% did not use non-financial monitors.	• Failure to monitor against external standards can lead to long-term loss of competitiveness. • Failure to monitor the non-financial factors that drive the financial performance results in a failure to manage them and to short-termism.
Evaluation of performance-monitoring information	• 42 to 63% were satisfied with the quality of the information they received, implying a significant minority were not. • However, 52% felt that critical issues were not highlighted.	• The results reflect a satisfaction with the quality of the internal financial information received.
Strategy formulation	• 76% measured the achievement of their objectives primarily against financial criteria.	• Over-emphasis on measuring strategic objectives against financial criteria results in losing sight of the underlying success factors, eg service.

Information	Key findings	Implications
External information for strategy formulation	● 42% on average used a lot of external information. ● Only 56% used competitor information frequently. ● Only 21% used information from their sales force and only 9% from their other employees.	● Failure to tap external sources of information will relegate strategy to slow and defensive/reactive.
Internal information for strategy formulation	● 73 to 81% used cost structure, product and past financial performance frequently. ● Only 56% used market-segment profitability information frequently. ● Only 33% used customer-profitability information frequently.	● Failure to use customer and segment profitability can result in wasted investments in developing customer accounts and segments, and the products and services that will satisfy them.
Analysis techniques	● 67% made decisions based on hunch/feeling. ● Only 23 to 32% used decision-support, econometric and EIS models.	● Failure to sufficiently analyse information can lead to the implications of information not being understood and poor decisions being made.
Evaluation of information for strategy formulation	● Up to 64% felt that the quality of such information was average, poor or very poor.	● Inadequate strategy-support information will lead to inferior strategies.

Data made usable is
Information when understood is
Knowledge when assimilated through action is
Experience when put into context provides
Insight when judiciously applied to provide
predictive capability is
Wisdom

PRINCIPLES OF POWER AND INFLUENCE

'... whether it is better to be loved than feared, or the reverse. The answer is that one would like to be both the one and the other; but because it is difficult to combine them, it is far better to be feared than loved if you cannot be both.'

Niccolo Machiavelli, *The Prince*

It is critically important to understand the different types of power and influence, and identify which key people in your organisation exercise them. Influence is the process whereby one modifies the attitudes or behaviour of another. Power is that which enables one to do it. Charles Handy in *Understanding Organisations* (Penguin, 1986) provides some useful categories of power:

- **Physical power** – the power of superior force
- **Resource or reward power** – the possession of valued resources
- **Position, legal or legitimate power** – arising from a role or position in the organisation giving the control over information, access and organisation
- **Expert power** – arising from acknowledged expertise
- **Personal power or charisma** – residing in the person and in his personality
- **Negative power** – the capacity to stop, delay, distort or disrupt things.

Handy points out that these bases of power allow influence of the following types to be exercised:

- **Force** – derived from physical power, it involves the application or threat of force
- **Rules and procedures** – used to influence everyone in a certain position to follow prescribed behaviour

- **Exchange** – bargaining, negotiating, cajoling or bribing usually exercised by those with resource or position power
- **Persuasion** – relies on logic, argument and evidence of the 'facts'
- **Ecology** – the use of the physical, psychological and sociological environment to influence individuals
- **Magnetism** – the application of personal power.

In order to understand an organisation it is necessary to understand the nature of power and influence, for they are the means by which objectives are achieved.

Information enables power and influence to be exercised effectively, because it reveals the existing power and influence bases and the extent to which these bases need to be utilised to achieve our purpose.

When the wider market and industrial context is considered the same principles apply. According to Professor Michael Porter of the Harvard Business School in his pioneering model of industry (*Competitive Strategy* (Harvard Free Press, 1980)), companies need information to assess the relative power of buyers, suppliers, rivals, potential rivals and product substitutes. In the light of this information they can adopt competitive positions. The power he refers to is the power to dictate terms and conditions and to thereby change the profitability of a market position.

The same principles apply to the wider macro-environment, both national and international. The question of the relative power of national bodies and international bodies, whether regulatory, governmental or lobbies, can determine the success or otherwise of an organisation's strategies. Therefore, information regarding the power and influence bases needs to be gathered as part of corporate strategy. The information required will be explored in more detail in Chapter Two. Your task is to ensure that power and influence are exercised in ways which are consistent with the values you seek to promote and meet the objectives you set.

IMPORTANCE OF INTELLIGENCE

In order to exercise power and influence you must have intelligence. In *The Art of War*, Sun Tzu points to the key strategic and tactical factors for winning wars. You will need intelligence to be able to achieve success in these factors:

Lay plans

'.. the general who wins a battle makes many calculations in his temple ere the battle is fought.'

Determine the implications, resources and sources needed to wage war

'It is only one who is thoroughly acquainted with the evils of war that can thoroughly understand the profitable ways of carrying it on.'

Attack by stratagem

'. . . to fight and conquer in all your battles is not supreme excellence; supreme excellence consists in breaking the enemy's resistance without fighting.'

Adopt tactics

'[We] first put ourselves beyond the possibility of defeat, and then wait[ed] for an opportunity of defeating the enemy.'

Deploy direct and indirect methods and create momentum in the use of one's forces

'The clever combatant looks to the effect of combined energy, and does not require too much from individuals.'

Exploit your rivals' strengths and weaknesses

'So in war, the way is to avoid what is strong and to strike at what is weak.'

Master the art of tactical manoeuvring

'The difficulty of tactical manoeuvring consists in turning the devious into the direct, and misfortune into gain.'

With regard to the importance of intelligence and counter-intelligence, Sun Tzu advised:

Know the conditions obtaining in the field

'*By means of seven considerations I can forecast victory or defeat.*'

These are described in Chapter Six, p 177 under 'Benchmarking'.

Present evidence to the enemy to deceive him

'*All warfare is based on deception.*'

Know yourself and your enemy along five strategic elements

'*Victory lies in the knowledge of these five points.*'

The five will be identified and explored in Chapter Five under 'Art of Opportunism'.

Deploy different spies for different purposes

'*Spies are a most important element in war, because on them depends an army's ability to move.*'

STRATEGY AND PLANNING

If you are to exercise power and influence, the intelligence gathered needs to be utilised in the formulation of strategy and the creation of business plans to steer the business.

A number of strategic planning frameworks exist and a large number of two-by-two matrices and grids have been developed by planners to provide insights into the strategic issues supporting strategy and planning. For example, the Boston Consulting Group's 'Growth-Share Matrix' was designed in 1977 as a guide to investing or divesting from a portfolio of business units. A variant of this was the 'General Electric Multifactor Portfolio Matrix' developed to make decisions to invest, divest or pursue earnings amongst a portfolio of businesses. Ansoff's 'Product/Market Expansion Grid' assists in the identification of new growth opportunities. The 'Product Life Cycle' plots sales and profits over time resulting in distinctive strategies between the phases of introduction, growth, maturity and decline. A vast number of such matrices can be developed, plotting any one variable against another, for example price v promotion, sales v advertising, product quality v market share, etc.

Figure 1 below provides a simple overall model for strategic planning.

Knowledge is the key driver of strategy. Strategy is the key driver of action plans.

Knowledge is required of:

- what the business is, what its strengths and weaknesses are, what its potential is, what its capacity to change is
- what the opportunities and threats facing the business are, what the capability of its rivals are, what the changing external environment holds for it
- what the business would like to be, how this relates to the knowledge of what it is and what the external environment means for it.

Strategy based on such knowledge is required to:

- determine where the business should go and how to take it there
- prepare the business for uncertainty
- prepare the business to seize opportunity
- prepare the business for change.

Figure 1 *Simplified strategic and business planning model*

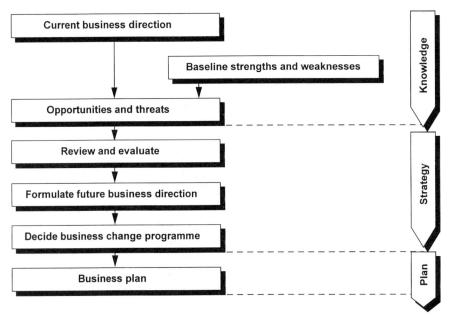

Plans are required to implement strategy and provide a detailed point of reference for the organisation to enable it to:

- prioritise efforts
- allocate resources to activities
- monitor progress.

The importance of systematically collecting information, formulating strategy and planning cannot be over-emphasised. Without the discipline of translating strategy into plans, your business will not effectively assimilate information, allocate resources, set targets, determine what does and does not work and have a reference point to compare its performance against and to decide whether to accept or reject opportunities. History provides some interesting examples of such a planning discipline carried to ruthless extremes.

Mongol campaigns were planned methodically. A general council would be called in which, while the actual decisions were undoubtedly made by Genghis Khan and a small group of trusted advisers, the lower-ranking officers might at least furnish information and receive their orders. Failure to attend was tantamount to suicide – those absent were subsequently killed. Possibly the most important part of this planning was the collection and evaluation of information concerning the enemy and his country. Spies were used, dissatisfied groups were identified, merchants of all nationalities provided information on roads and officials who could be bribed, and traitors and opposition groups were encouraged.

The essential difference between effective and ineffective leadership is the ability to use your power and influence to put your plans into action.

THE SCIENCE OF OMNISCIENCE

A business cannot know everything there is to know about itself, its rivals and its environment; it cannot be omniscient. So what is the 'science of omniscience'? It is the systematic acquisition and assimilation of all the relevant information to provide everything a business wants to know, when and where it wants it. The sharedealer sitting in front of a set of screens with the right technical and analytical support comes fairly close to the science:

- **everything a business wants to know** – the share prices, volumes of trade, relevant economic, competitive, political and media information, latest share movements, trends, identity of the initiators of trades, etc
- **systematically acquired** – by third parties and people in the front-line of news, in the backroom collecting and filtering, in the computer room transmitting the information to the dealer
- **assimilated to provide knowledge** – analysed by third parties, by the business and by the dealer
- **available real time** – immediate electronic updates of information on screen from multiple sources, seconds or minutes after it happens
- **where it is wanted** – in the office, at the desk, on screen.

Can the situation of the sharedealer be re-created in a business environment? This is getting closer to becoming attainable. The cost of such information acquisition and management is decreasing as technology advances; in parallel, specialist information acquisition companies are able to spread their costs, and profit requirements, across a large number of customers.

But what would such a system cost an organisation? The cost depends on the following factors:

- the underlying **complexity** of the business, which increases with the number of subsidiaries, national and international spread, products, markets and customers, suppliers, technologies and organisational hierarchies
- the **decisions** that need to be made and the information required to support such decisions
- the **speed** with which such information is required
- the degree to which such information can be used 'raw' and the extent to which **value addition** is necessary through processing, modelling and analysis

- the proliferation of **systems** across the business, their acquisition of critical information, their speed of processing and their integration and ability to communicate with each other
- the degree of human **manual interaction** to compensate for gaps in the business systems
- the degree to which existing **external information** agents exist, are reliable and the cost of links with them.

So how does a business go about creating the omniscient system? The subject of this book is the creation of such a system. By the final chapter the answer will be apparent.

Technological advances are bringing closer the creation of such learning and assimilating systems. While the current applications are restricted and based on improving process performance, the potential is enormous.

In a study of 100 US manufacturing companies across all sectors, it was found that the use of 'knowledge-based' technology to emulate human thought processes and create flexible, artificially intelligent manufacturing tools provided quantified process-performance advantages. For example:

- At Northcorp Aircraft time was cut for the design and manufacturing process of machine parts from 12 hours to 15 minutes
- At Campbell Soup diagnostic tools at manufacturing sites allowed the engineering staff at cooking sites to be reduced
- At IBM knowledge-based systems for the testing of disk drives saved $18 million a year. This was just one of 180 examples of the use of such systems in IBM.

Source: M. Oliff and R. Collies, 'Expert Systems: the bridge to intelligent manufacturing' *Imede Perspective for Managers*, no 5, 1989.

Throughout this process it would be well to remember the analogy of Sun Tzu leading the Ancient Chinese army of the Kingdom of Wu or Alexander the Great traversing from Greece through Egypt, Afghanistan and India – the terrain, the foe, the heavens and our army change. And as they change, our information requirements change too. A static assessment is soon out of date in the ever-changing world, so unless we are aware of what is going on around us and amend our information needs accordingly, we cannot hope to win in a changing world. Chapter Six examines how such 'moving pictures' are constructed.

SOURCES OF INFORMATION

The ability to get hold of relevant information is uncertain; it is easier in some industries than others. The types of information available are given in Figure 2 below.

Figure 2   *Information sources*

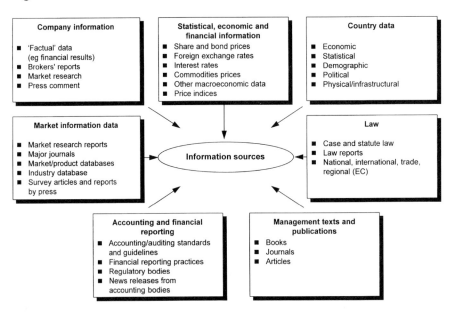

As a leader you must create a wide range of information sources. In this chapter we will outline the conventional ones; in later chapters the more unconventional will also be examined. The conventional sources of such information are:

- **Data-modelling companies** such as the Henley Management Centre, especially for the macro environment, and PIMS (Profit Impact of Market Strategy) provide a benchmarking service based on peer-group comparison
- Industry-specific comparisons are often carried out by **management consultants, industry and trade associations**. Such groups often act as information brokers and can provide the specific information on operations, processes and activities required to make change
- **Information groups** such as Jordans, ICC and Mintel provide detailed financial comparisons
- Rivals and non-rivals regularly reveal information regarding their performance through the **media**, via press releases, interviews and authored articles. A business can use this information to create its own benchmarking database
- Many companies will allow non-rivals to visit their businesses and discuss their practices and the lessons they have learnt. KPMG, for example, has arranged such **discussions** for its own clients. In considering whether and in what form to set up its internal operational review group, KPMG arranged for Nuclear Electric to visit Hewlett Packard and National Westminster Bank
- You may find that your rivals are not as careful as you might imagine about who they allow to **visit** their facilities. The Japanese may thank the West for the welcome they received in the 1970s when they visited its automotive, machine tools, electronics and consumer goods factories in search of learning and comparison.

IN THIS CHAPTER_____

We have begun to define the nature of the strategist. We found that the first fundamental challenge is to exercise power and influence. To achieve this the leader requires knowledge. Using this knowledge, the leader can begin to plan how he will achieve his objective. The depth and breadth of information required in this context has also been briefly explored. The principles of the chapter are summarised in Figure 3 below.

Figure 3 *Knowledge, power and influence*

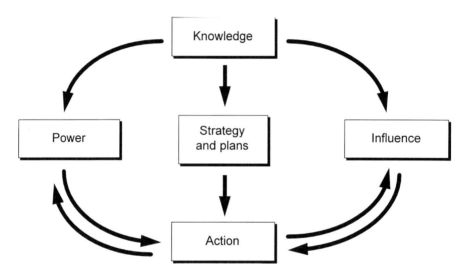

In the coming chapters these themes will be built on, beginning with the macro-environment, before moving on to consider how information can be used by a business to get to know itself and its enemy, and to determine its position. There is then an illustration of how this information can be used in attack, defence and tactical manoeuvring. Finally, all the themes in this book will be drawn together to demonstrate how they can be used to create an information machine for managing and transforming businesses.

LEADERSHIP CHALLENGE
TWO

Decide how to benefit from and become the architect of macro-change

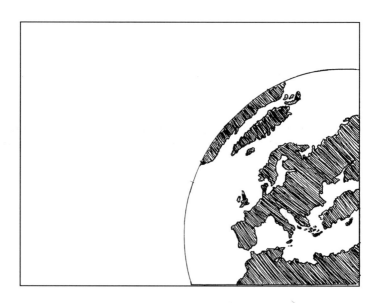

Chapter Two

MACRO-ENVIRONMENT: KNOW THE WORLD

'We are not fit to lead an army on the march unless we are familiar with the face of the country – its mountains and forests, its pitfalls and precipices, its marshes and swamps.'

Sun Tzu, *The Art of War*, fifth century BC

INTRODUCTION

So much of the outcome of an organisation's strategies, tactics and plans appears to be outside its control; the passive acceptance of this perception results in most companies becoming the victims of wider macro-level forces. In this chapter, the ground will be prepared for the rest of the book, and the need to put aside such perceptions will be demonstrated, showing instead that the understanding of its environment can allow a business to seize opportunities and perhaps even mould the environment itself to the organisation's advantage. Through the use of examples, this chapter explores the importance of macro-level information to the success of corporate strategies and examines how some companies and individuals have become victims of the environment while others have made their own 'luck'.

We begin by taking a look at the role that you, the leader, must play to meet the challenge. Napoleon provides an example of how to achieve world domination.

MEETING CHALLENGE TWO

To meet the leadership challenge you must demonstrate the ability to shape the main macro-forces driving your industry. The key leadership quality to meet this challenge is **visualisation**, which requires:

- foresight – the ability to predict what will happen, and
- imagination – the ability to see the scenarios that *could* happen.

The key leadership quality to implement visualisation is **relationship management**. Of particular importance is game planning and game playing.

Leadership entails significant responsibilities. These include ensuring that:

- information on the world is systematically captured
- this information is used to seek out the key drivers, trends and relationships between macro-forces
- a vision of the future is formed to predict likely and potential outcomes; and
- opportunities are identified to shape the forces and thereby shape the industry outcome.

If you cannot discharge these responsibilities you will relegate your organisation to following, not leading – and not by design, but by default.

NAPOLEON (1769–1821)

Napoleon represents a modern leader who had a grand vision of the way he wanted his world to be and took on the task of shaping the world to his vision. Napoleon crossed national boundaries and became a legend. A generation after his death, when Queen Victoria visited his tomb in Paris she instructed her son, the future King Edward VII, to 'Kneel down before the tomb of the great Napoleon'.

Napoleon was born in Corsica, educated in Paris and at the age of 16 was commissioned as second lieutenant of artillery. He rose up through the ranks and in 1796 took command of the French Army in Italy. In the next 5 years he was victorious in Italy, conquered Egypt, and became first consul of France. In 1803, only the English agitated against him. In 1804, he was declared the emperor of the French. Over the next few years, he continued his domination of nations by prevailing over Russia, Austria, Prussia and Spain. The English continued to disrupt his empire and by 1812 the Russians had mustered armies for war.

In 1812, Napoleon led an army of over 500,000 drawn from all over Europe into Russia in a pre-emptive attack. Instead of challenging him, the Russians retreated to lure him further inland. The march was a disaster. His supplies ran out and the Russians burnt their crops as they retreated. Thousands of troops deserted in hunger and despair. Napoleon reached Moscow and after 10 hours of fighting with the Russian army he prevailed. The people of Moscow failed to co-operate with him and fled to the countryside. The winter set in and Napoleon ordered his army to retreat. A demoralised army travelled back through snow and cold, and Napoleon lost 400,000 men from starvation, minor attacks, exhaustion, cold and disease. After winning so many battles in his career, Napoleon had lost by failing to keep good lines of supply and through reckless ambition.

Over the next year or two the emperor's supporters and allies deserted him and in 1814 his enemies forced his abdication. Napoleon was given the little island of Elba. Meanwhile the rulers in France failed to manage their affairs. Napoleon once more took power and fought the English and the Prussians and came close to winning. Finally defeated at Waterloo, he was imprisoned in St Helena in the South Atlantic where he died in 1821.

Napoleon had reigned as one of the great emperors of the modern world. Reflecting on his life, he exclaimed, 'After all, what a romance my life has been!' He crossed organised national boundaries and altered frontiers in a way that no one else had in a millennium. He gave France his Code which is still the basis of French law. Across the nations that he ruled he instituted basic human rights, freedom of belief and public infrastructures. A builder rather than a destroyer, he left behind harbours, roads, bridges and canals. He practised meritocracy in placing his staff and ruled as a civilian not a military leader. He warred within an overall strategic plan and with a clear mission. He understood how to seize the advantage and how to create the conditions for success. His mobilisation, equipping and training of mass resources marked the beginning of modern warfare. He was a master at fighting battles and manoeuvring. He had the ability to sustain his troop's morale and to inspire them to extraordinary feats. In action he was fearless and after the battle he looked after his men. His mistakes were spectacular and came from over-confidence and a desperate need to keep the world at bay.

Napoleon's dazzling make-up – combining ego, a craving for power, vision, a romantic nature, the capacity for hard work, and the ability to motivate and lead – enabled him to shape the world around him.

MACRO-LEVEL INFORMATION

It is critically important to understand the macro-level environment around you so that you can determine how best to shape it and gain from it. The framework for analysis of the macro-level environment is given in Figure 4 below.

Definitions

Macro-economics
The macro-economic environment is created by the interaction of output, consumption and income. The outcome of this interaction is also affected by factors such as inflation, interest rates, trade and balance of payments.

Physical and infrastructural
The physical environment is the set of natural resources and landscape of a country. Infrastructure is built into this environment by man to enable habitation, exploitation and transportation of resources.

Figure 4   *The macro-level environment – forces at play on the company's internal environment*

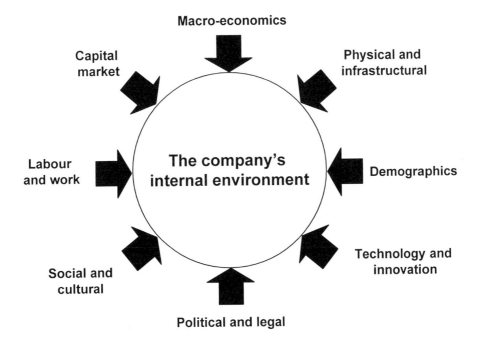

Demographics
The demographic environment is determined by the characteristics of the population of a country.

Technology and innovation
The technological environment is that resulting from man's innovation in creating solutions to cope better with his environment.

Political and legal
The political and legal environment is made up of all the statutory and regulatory compliance requirements.

Social and cultural
The socio-cultural environment is a result of the mix of beliefs, assumptions, values, attitudes and norms of the people in society.

Labour and work
The labour and working environment is a subset of the economic environment, focusing on the characteristics of the work force.

Capital market
The capital market environment is the availability of funds and the form in which funds are available to finance ventures.

HOW TO USE SUCH HIGH-LEVEL INFORMATION

Winners and losers
There are those that will be buffeted by the changing environment around them and those that will change the environment to suit themselves. For macro-economic information to be of any use, a business needs to translate it into what it means for its own industry and for the organisation's position within that industry. The macro-level factors are often judged by companies to be outside their control: Napoleon said that 'War is composed of nothing but accidents' and that 'luck' was the ability to exploit these chance accidents.

Your interest in the macro-environment is encapsulated in the following two questions:

- **Can you influence the outcome?**
- **Can you act to avoid risk or benefit from the outcome?**

Most businesses act in ignorance of the macro-environmental factors; many do not insure themselves against risks such as fluctuations in exchange rates and interest rates. However, there are some spectacular examples of businesses and individuals influencing the outcome of strategies and benefiting from not leaving the result to Napoleon's chance.

In 1992 the will of the British Government and its European partners in attempting to maintain the European Exchange Rate Mechanism was pitted against that of thousands of small traders across the world. At a certain moment, a perception of the inevitable collapse of the pound became widely held by both sides. In creating this perception the key factors were:

- the use of millions of pounds by one trader in a calculated gamble to influence the outcome
- the regular coverage by the media of the view of informed groups of economists as the inevitability of the collapse of sterling
- the real-time information at the finger-tips of the traders making buy and sell decisions
- the lack of power evident in the actions and words of European politicians.

This information was used by many, but the situation was created and spectacularly manipulated and exploited by one man, George Soros, to bring down the pound and thereby to profit by $1 billion. He bet that despite strong statements from the British Government to the contrary, Britain would abandon the European Exchange Rate Mechanism rather than continually defend the pound through expensive interventions in the currency markets. He was dubbed by Fleet Street as the man who 'broke the Bank of England'.

The vision to interpret

The task of the leader is to ensure that the organisation develops an insight into the factors that will allow it to take the initiative in its industry, namely:

- the immediate impact of current macro-level forces
- the key industry trends that will shape the future of the industry
- the key drivers or determinants of each trend
- the potential future scenarios.

These factors allow you to decide how to shape the future of your industry, how to benefit from macro-level changes and how to avoid unnecessary risk.

The macro-environmental information needs to be combined to see the future cocktail of opportunity. A business cannot look at the economic, political or socio-cultural factors in isolation: a pattern has to be discerned. In Chapter Six the principles upon which such a picture can be built are discussed.

General Electric (GE) has shown great vision and determination in its global strategy. A 1993 analysis of the recent eco-political situation in India reveals about 500 million people living below European poverty levels, sporadic sectarian violence and anti-foreign agitation which has forced some Western companies to abandon their ventures: for example, Cargill dropped out of a major salt-mining operation and Envon's major energy project was publicly discredited and disowned by local government. However, Jack Welch, chief executive officer of GE, sees the future of GE in India, China and Mexico. GE has invested $100 million in factories for manufacturing plastics, kitchen appliances, medical imaging equipment and lamps, and achieved sales of $444 million. The company faces 3% overall growth in its combined business. GE believes that its future lies in such mass markets and that the conditions of the present cannot guide future strategy. It estimates that 25% of revenues ($20 billion) in the year 2000 will come from these three countries.

Source: M. Oliff and R. Collies, 'GE's brave new world' *Business Week*, 8 November 1993.

MACRO-ECONOMICS

Macro-economic forces are likely to be beyond the influence of most businesses, who are therefore often at the mercy of national and increasingly international governmental decisions.

The theory

Figure 5 below provides an outline of a macro-economic model for determining the factors affecting the economy. In this simplistic model the impact of imports and exchange rates have not been explicitly drawn out.

Figure 5 *Simple macro-economic model*

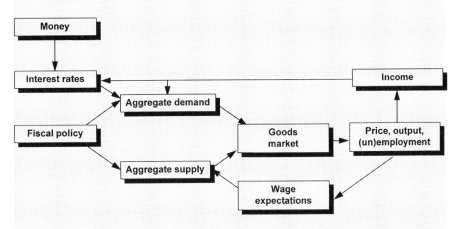

Source: Dornbusch and Fischer, *Macroeconomics* (McGraw-Hill, 1981). Reproduced by permission of The McGraw-Hill Companies © 1981.

The model presents, in simple terms, the relationship between the major macro-economic variables. Underlying the model are a number of assumptions regarding the relationships between each of these variables and their underlying causes, for example the behaviour of people in matters such as their propensity to spend or save and speculative expenditure, the relationship between income and employment and the stability of prices and money supply. This book does not concern itself with the complexities, theories and counter-theories of macro-economists. Instead, it focuses on the information needed and how it can be used to influence business performance.

Information needs

We can get a reasonable feel for the key factors affecting business by looking at measures indicating the attitudes of and results of decisions by:

- consumers, for example savings, debt and expenditure patterns, and unemployment
- government, for example inflation, interest rates, exchange rates, expenditure levels, taxation, monetary policy
- businesses, for example pay settlements, investment, growth, output
- supplier and customer nations, for example relative inflation, interest rates, prices, export and import patterns.

Lessons to be learned from the use of macro-economic information

In examining such information you must ask yourself:

- what the future demand for products will be
- what the future supply for products will be
- what price can be expected and how sensitive demand and supply are to price
- what the impact will be of decisions made by the organisation's governments and by its suppliers' and customers' governments.

The changing economic cycle presents a range of opportunities for entrepreneurs and creates pressure for larger, more established businesses to adjust their prices and performance. In the UK, Amber Day, a small cut-price clothing company, opened a shop to take advantage of the demand for low-price clothes in the recession of the late 1980s and early 1990s. Burtons adopted a 'discount pricing' strategy involving ad hoc 'Blue Cross' days, where prices would be reduced for the day by 10 to 30%. Seasonal price reductions in the Burton Group seemed to last all year round with Christmas sales running into spring, summer and then autumn sales. The Savoy Tailor's Guild had the fortune or misfortune of finding 'The Discount Shop' only about a hundred yards along the Strand, with shirts advertised in bold in the main windows for about £3.99. To save recessionary pressures, the upmarket brand businesses were forced to offer consumers greater value either by offering unique styling and fabrics or by cutting the prices of their branded products.

Your leadership challenge is not only to predict the impact on your organisation of the economic cycle, but also to help your organisation decide what new price-performance opportunities should be created as a result of economic downturns and upturns.

PHYSICAL AND INFRASTRUCTURAL INFORMATION

Information needs
The key information regarding the physical and infra-structural environment includes:

- the availability of raw materials
- location, availability and cost of energy
- the state of the environment and the controls in place
- availability and suitability of roads, airways, waterways and transportation.

Lessons to be learned from the use of physical and infrastructural information
Information regarding the physical and infrastructural environment should be examined to discern whether location provides any advantages and whether the country in which the business intends to trade has the physical infrastructure to enable trade to take place.

In the 1970s and early 1980s economic theory focused on comparative advantages, ie those advantages accruing to companies due to their physical location. The scope of these advantages included low labour costs that accrued to Far East Asia.

In the mid- to late 1980s the importance of comparative advantage was overtaken by the theory of competitive advantages, ie those created by a company or available to it due to the structure of the industry. It was argued that, relatively, it mattered less where companies such as Apple, Hewlett Packard or Volkswagen were located: they would succeed because they secured their advantage from such factors as the productivity of their people, technological advances, the rate of innovation, timing and speed to market. The rise of Japanese companies in the high-wage Japanese economy was used to justify the theory.

More balanced analysis of course pointed to a mix of factors, including exchange rates, government industrial strategy, low borrowing interest rates and indeed the availability of a malleable working population. The competitive advantage proponents' contentions were often contrary to the actions of some of these companies, who, believing in their competitive advantages, still chose locations that yielded them the greatest comparative advantages such as government subsidies and an educated labour force.

In the 1990s, with the firm establishment of competitive advantages such as the entry criteria for competing in global markets and the hunger for further means of gaining advantages, we are seeing the resurgence of comparative advantage as an important decision factor, evidenced by:

- global competitors choosing to locate their factories in low-cost European nations such as the UK, parts of France and Eastern Europe
- an influx of companies into China utilising the vastly superior productivity and work ethic of the southern Chinese
- the location of chemical plants in Third World countries due to the poor environmental controls tolerated by their governments and the consequent lack of a need to invest in expensive emission reduction and neutralisation equipment.

These companies are no doubt attracted by the need to locate within the country in order to tap the local market demand. However, the companies find that the comparative advantages offered by these countries also enable them to export from these locations to their global markets.

DEMOGRAPHICS

Information needs

Demographic information is important in determining potential market size and characteristics. At a macro-level the key information is:

- population and population density
- geographic distribution
- mobility of population
- age distribution
- birth, marriage and death statistics
- racial, ethnic and religious breakdown
- education and occupational breakdown.

Lessons to be learned from the use of demographic information

This macro-analysis only becomes useful in marketing strategy if a business can address such questions as:

- What attributes should its product have to attract customers
- What should it do to attract these customers
- How many people will be attracted to buy its products
- How much will they be willing to pay
- Where will they wish to buy from?

This is the basis of marketing-mix analysis. The macro-level information can be coupled with more specific information on customer preferences to address the above questions using market segmentation analysis. The use of segmentation will be examined in the next chapter.

TECHNOLOGY AND INNOVATION

Information needs

Technology is increasingly recognised as a key driver of change and performance. The key macro-level information includes:

- the pace of technological innovation
- new discoveries
- the size of R & D budgets
- the focus on incremental development
- the regulations covering the introduction of innovative products.

Lessons to be learned from the use of technology and innovation information

These global changes in technology and innovation can help business strategy if the organisation can determine and secure:

- the commercial applications of the innovations
- the economic introduction of such innovations
- their favourable impact on existing products, customers and processes.

Post-war Japan and 1970s Korea and Singapore illustrate the need to focus on quality and technology. These countries had been low-quality producers with low investment in technology; they realised that securing a share of the global market required them to not only match but to leap-frog their Western rivals on technology investment. This began with investments to copy and later improve processes and methods, then moved to a stream of continuous investments to develop the product itself, and then to research in the basic technologies underlying the processes and products to beat their countries' rivals. An understanding of this pattern allows us to forecast the developments that are due to come from India and China over the next decade.

POLITICAL AND LEGAL INFORMATION

Information needs
The key information includes:

- legislation to regulate business
- the objectives, scope, power and intent of regulatory bodies
- the influence of lobbying groups
- the mix and transference of ownership between government and the individual
- government policy regarding the promotion of specific markets.

Lessons to be learned from the use of political and legal information
Political and legal information can be of use if the business can determine factors such as:

- what the likely government or legislative agenda is
- what the consequences are for the number of entrants, competition, pricing and other factors affecting profitability
- how the business can assist the government to achieve its agenda
- how the business can influence the government agenda, for example through lobbying and participation in industry interest group and think tanks.

Governments will often introduce trade barriers, build infrastructure, forgo taxes, provide cheap capital, fund training, and subsidise employment costs if your enterprise fits their agenda. Your leadership challenge is to understand their agenda and gain maximum benefits from the overlap with yours.

In the early 1980s, the British Government commenced an ambitious programme of privatisation. After a first attempt to privatise the North Sea gas fields, for which the Government was bitterly criticised for transferring a public monopoly to private hands, it proceeded with the privatisation of the electricity industry. The key information of interest to a number of businesses included the answers to the following questions:

- What were the Government's key motivating factors and what would make its objectives saleable to the British public? If this could be determined, a company could position itself to assist the Government in achieving its objectives. For example, if the Government wished to create a competitive environment, a large new entrant could secure incentives that would damage the existing players and enhance its own profitability.
- How would the industry be structured and what would the resulting industry profitability be? If the structure of the industry featured much high-cost capacity which would be damaged in favour of low-cost capacity, then a programme of early divestment and investment could be favoured.
- What were the existing players' competencies in functions such as marketing, systems and finance? If these were inadequate for the future environment then a large consultancy market existed for preparing the incumbents for the new world.

The answers to these and many other questions enabled a large number of businesses – management consultants, financiers, marketing advisers and power generators – to make millions of pounds.

SOCIAL AND CULTURAL INFORMATION

Information needs
The key information required to determine the influence of the socio-cultural environment is the nature of:

- the core cultural values
- the subcultures existing within the society
- the temporary 'fads' that influence the culture.

Lessons to be learned from the use of socio-cultural information

This information becomes critical to strategy when the business can answer precise questions regarding:

- what the finely divided consumer segments within the core culture and the subcultures are
- how the organisation's proposition fits within the value system of its target market segments
- how the marketing mix of its product creates, influences and satisfies the 'fads'
- what the cultural influences upon the business are in terms of corporate as well as national cultures.

The restructuring of the back office and the creation of shared service centres across national and subsidiary boundaries is one of the emerging themes for international corporations in the Western world. A number of significant cultural and social issues need to be faced before giving too much weight to the 'rational' arguments. Examples include:

- Is an Italian finance director still a powerful and influential figure if his function is reduced from 50 to 10 staff in the post-rationalised scenario? If he is not, then how will strong financial control continue to be exercised?
- Will Portugal's customers be happy being serviced by a centre placed in Spain or vice versa? A number of such national differences and attitudes need to be taken into account.
- How will customers in the Republic of Ireland feel if the person answering debt queries in the shared service centre speaks with a Northern Irish accent?

As much weight needs to be given to the cultural, political and emotional considerations as to the economic considerations.

LABOUR AND WORK INFORMATION

Information needs

The key information required at a macro-level is:

- the supply of labour across regions
- the power of the workforce relative to the employer

- the mix of skills, experience and length of service of the labour force
- the productivity (cost versus output) of the workforce
- the work ethic of the people.

Lessons to be learned from the use of labour and work information

For this information to be useful the business needs more precise information for each region, and an assessment of the workforce's aptitude and how flexible and amenable it is to the organisation's way of working.

In the run up to European integration in 1992, decisions on the location of businesses across Europe focused on a number of key business issues – environment, costs, market size and resources. The availability of skilled labour and, in particular educated and skilled management was a key concern due to the immobility of labour across national boundaries and especially from northern to southern Europe. Statistical analysis revealed some interesting information: the labour force across the 12 EC countries was 126 million, compared to 123 million in the US and 63 million in Japan. Of this EC population, 71% was situated in France, the former West Germany, Italy and the UK; only 7.5% was located in Greece, Ireland, Luxembourg and Portugal. Companies considering setting up business in Europe often looked at the potential future labour supply and found that:

- in the 16- to 18-year-old age group the UK and Spain were lagging behind the rest, ie had the smaller workforce
- for those aged 18-plus, Germany, the Netherlands, Belgium and Denmark had 67 to 80% of their population in further education. The UK had only 42%, of which just 20% were in full-time education.

Source: *Multinational Business*, 1990/91, no 4.

Macro-analysis is useful in location strategy to answer questions such as 'Are the required resources, numbers, skills and other attributes available to enable the business to operate effectively?' The leadership task is to determine how to align management and staff to meet the competitive challenge, how to get the best from your people and how to make work a fun place to be.

In achieving such aims, the global trends in the workplace are of relevance to your business. The factors driving the nature of the workplace include the size of the workforce, its organisation into divisions and hierarchies, the skills of the people, their focus and orientation, the time they put into the job and the way the business treats them and helps them to develop.

Table 2 *Illustration of global workplace trends*

Characteristics	Present	Future
Size	Large	Small
Structure	Hierarchical	Network
Skills	Manufacturing	Service
Delivery focus	Product	Service
Orientation	Task	Learning/problem solving
Time input	9am to 5pm	Continuous
Controllers	Managers	Coach/mentor

Table 2 above illustrates the possibility that more global changes in the workplace may force a business to respond more radically than it anticipated. The UK has so far resisted the working-practice changes of the other northern European members of the European Union but may find itself forced to change due to competitive pressures long before a form of words is agreed with its European partners.

CAPITAL MARKET INFORMATION

Information needs

The key information required on the capital market is:

- the amount of freedom in the flow of international funds
- the credibility of the banking industry and the degree of inter-bank competition
- the presence of an international stock exchange consisting of the country's largest companies
- the presence of secondary stock markets for smaller companies
- the presence of other funding institutions

- the integrity of financial-service institutions and stock exchanges, determined by the regulatory environment
- the cost of capital and how that varies with risk and return profiles
- the availability of instruments to hedge risks and fund trade.

Lessons to be learned from the use of capital market information

This information needs to be distilled to assess:

- whether financial institutions will lend you money
- what their terms and conditions will be
- what other services are available to help smooth business transactions
- what is happening in the market and what is about to happen: often a presence is required just to understand the movements in foreign markets.

The CEO's and CFO's challenge is to sustain good shareholder relations, deliver share-value growth and dividends and secure low-cost capital to fund their strategies.

During the 1990s there has been a growing realisation in Western Europe that the 'great potential' of India is about to become a reality. A decade earlier the Japanese, Americans and Australians had sown the seeds for their success, many of them in the infrastructure sectors including the capital markets. Many of the world's major banking institutions had long provided corporate finance and share-dealing services: some of the prominent players included GE, Capital Citibank, HSBC and ANZ Grindlays. Most of the European banks and financial institutions were late to recognise the eminence of the Indian market because of the poorly developed and poorly regulated capital and economic markets. Many European businesses were waiting for India to meet Western criteria for attractiveness: established credit-rating agencies, better stock exchange regulation and reliable physical infrastructure were amongst their key requirements. In 1994, the stock market boomed and the Indian and established foreign players made extravagant profits. Many of the Western European players entered the market just as those in the know started to take profits and the market collapsed.

IN THIS CHAPTER_____

We have examined the types of macro-level information required by business. Such information has been demonstrated to be the basic ingredient which, combined with vision, will enable a business to handle the forces of the 'heavens'. Your leadership challenge is to use this information to allow your business to be the master of its own destiny. The principles of the chapter are summarised in Figure 6 below.

Figure 6   *Macro-environment: know the world around you*

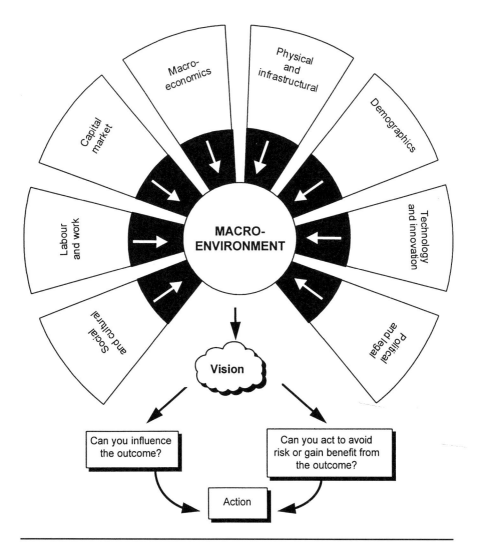

The next chapter goes one step forward by examining how information regarding an organisation's position and that of its rivals can be used as the basis for securing and creating superior positions for the business.

LEADERSHIP CHALLENGE
THREE

Develop insight into the capabilities and flaws of your organisation, your rivals and your competitive battlegrounds

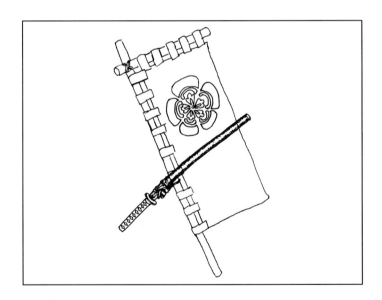

Chapter Three

DETERMINING POSITION: KNOW YOURSELF, YOUR ENEMY AND YOUR POSITION

'If you know the enemy and know yourself, you need not fear the result of a hundred battles. If you know yourself but not the enemy, for every victory gained you will also suffer a defeat. If you know neither the enemy nor yourself, you will succumb in every battle ... if you know Heaven and Earth, you may make your victory complete.'

Sun Tzu, *The Art of War*

INTRODUCTION

Sun Tzu's guidance and the lack of information regarding business 'enemies' indicated in the KPMG-commissioned Harris survey (see pp 12–13) provide one clue as to why many companies are failing in the increasingly competitive markets of today. The identity, motives and commitment of business rivals are often a mystery; they adopt positions and tactics that cannot be fathomed; they are found 'cherry-picking' attractive niches and undercutting prices. In frustration, many chief executive officers wonder if their rivals are destroying the market, buying market share or are simply far cleverer than themselves. Without information and a method for processing it the competitive puzzle cannot be solved.

This chapter will examine what it is that a business needs to know about itself, its enemies and its position. We will begin by taking a look at the role that you, the leader, must play to meet the challenge. The lesson in creating positions from which you can win comes from Tokugawa Ieyasu.

MEETING CHALLENGE THREE

To meet the leadership challenge you must demonstrate the ability to shape your organisation, your rivals and your situation. The key leadership quality to meet this challenge is again **visualisation**, which requires:

- the ability to read the situation
- a deep insight into people's motivation and the ability to put yourself in others' shoes
- foresight (predictive capability), and
- the imagination to see the scenarios that *could* happen.

The key leadership quality required to implement visualisation is **relationship management**. Of great importance will be the attributes of:

- game planning and game playing
- toughness in action and thought, and
- the ability to shape people's expectations.

Leadership entails significant responsibilities. These include ensuring that:

- information on your organisation, rivals and situation is systematically captured
- this information is used to understand your and your rival's capabilities and intent
- a prediction is formed of the likely situations and the competitive implications
- the opportunities to create and take advantage of new situations are identified.

If you cannot discharge these responsibilities you will confine your organisation to operating in market situations and sectors created, led and exploited by others.

TOKUGAWA IEYASU (1543–1616)

In the last of the traditional pre-modern eras of Japan came the Edo or Tokugawa period. In reference to the relative contribution of three great unifiers in the samurai history of Japan, the old Japanese saying goes 'Nobunaga piled the rice, Hideyoshi kneaded the dough, while Tokugawa Ieyasu ate the cake'.

Ieyasu was a samurai. The first 20 years of his life were spent as a hostage. In this period, he learnt court politics as well as the samurai art of fighting. He had served under Nobunaga and then Hideyoshi. Once the great Hideyoshi was dead, Ieyasu moved to seize power. His rival was Ishida Mitsunari of West Japan. Ieyasu's chosen battleground was Sekigahara, the most strategically placed crossroads in Japan. To this end, he cleverly threatened Ishida's lines of communication to the east and drew him to the crossroads where he defeated him. Ieyasu became Shogun. However, in 1614, Hideyoshi's son mustered supporters and held out in Osaka Castle against him. Ieyasu lay siege and through trickery finally drew the enemy out into a battle which he won.

Ieyasu had a clear understanding of the situation based on 50 years of samurai experience under some of Japan's great leaders. He quickly implemented a masterful plan to secure his immediate and long-term position. His plan had five elements to it. The first was to ensure that there would be no strongholds requiring siege tactics to defeat them ever again: he ordered and realised in days the destruction of all non-residential castles in Japan. The second was to follow through and ensure the disarming of all non-samurai classes, thereby limiting the ability of the people to rebel. Thirdly, Ieyasu ensured that there would be no rebellion from the samurai class. All those that had opposed him at Osaka were given fiefs at the outskirts of Japan and all his supporters were given surrounding fiefs. The fourth measure was to extend the attendance system to require all nobles to live in Edo every other year and to house their wives and children there permanently. This annual change of residence combined with compulsory donations served as a means of impoverishing many of his possible rivals. His power enabled him to enforce this hostage taking. Finally, Ieyasu centralised the production, licensing and procurement of firearms and cannon. He understood the Japanese sword culture and made firearms the enemy of the noble fighter.

Ieyasu had a masterful understanding of the current and possible future situations that could threaten his position. He seized the opportunity, defeated the enemy quickly, learned well and implemented thoroughly. He had vision and determination and shaped the future of Japan by not only controlling his armed forces but by limiting the movement of his possible rivals. His weapons were military, economic and cultural. As a result of the conditions he created and enforced, his family ruled Japan as Shoguns for two and a half centuries.

KNOW YOURSELF

Your first task is to understand your organisation's capabilities and limitations. This capability is strategic if a business has combined its resources in such a way as to create a unique position in an area of importance to its market endeavours which cannot be easily copied by its rivals. The critical information required concerns the inherent strengths and weaknesses of:

- **the bank of resources** – men, machines, money, materials
- **the products and services**
- **the coverage** – channels and intermediaries, geographic areas, market segments, customers, consumers
- **the core competencies** – technological, managerial, etc. Hamel and Prahalad in their reference work on core competencies describe Sony's core competence of miniaturisation as the basis of its success in making the Walkman, video cameras and notebook computers. This work has been taken to the next level in *Competing for the Future* (Harvard Business School Press, 1994)
- **the strategic capabilities** – unique value system or business process advantages built through investments combining technology, people and organisation. Honda's core competencies in engines and power trains enabled it to make lawn mowers, boat motors, cars and motor bikes. However, it was this competence combined with the building of operational strengths such as management of dealers and fast product development that enabled it to create a lead over its rivals in each of the above product markets. The creation of such supply-chain differentials is what is referred to as strategic capabilities
- **the alliances and collaborations** – with suppliers, customers and within the business.

Cargill provides an excellent example of a company that has worked out its competencies and uses them as the basis for its expansionary strategy. Cargill merchandises, processes and transports agricultural and other commodities. It also produces fertilisers, flour, corn syrup and salt. In addition, it processes steel, fabricates wire products, sells poultry entrees and imports shrimps, and provides financial trading and brokerage services. This sounds like a diverse and unrelated set of activities. What links them together? What is the commercial logic?

The answer is that the exploitation of opportunities is based on core competencies. Cargill is clear that its core competencies are the handling of commodities, risk management, transportation, basic processing and financial expertise in evaluating commodities markets. These are its transferable competencies and the basis on which the diverse opportunities have been exploited.

The key information regarding each of the above areas should be evaluated to establish:

- the prima facie strengths and weaknesses, for example quality, cost, volume, throughput, cycle time
- the profitability of activities for example product or customer profitability
- the shortfall from benchmarks, for example comparison to industry norms, 'best of breed' or rivals'
- the adequacy of financial performance, for example asset utilisation, return on capital employed, debtor turnover.

The above are the 'physical' aspects. The business also needs to know the strengths and weaknesses of its 'psychological' make-up:

- the management commitment to its vision and strategy
- the commitment of its people to the corporate mission
- the flexibility of its people and their willingness to embrace fast change
- the motivation of its people to innovate and learn
- the shared commitment of its allies to the joint cause.

The easiest information to collect should be about the business itself. However, most large organisations will admit that they know nowhere near as much as they should about their own business. Some of the key reasons contributing to this myopia include:

- **business diversity and distance from front line** – as the product range, customer type, physical location and variety of distribution outlets increase the 'head office' strategist becomes the armchair strategist
- **bureaucracy in data collection** – the information providers in such organisations are often six layers removed from the recipients and the process of collection, filtration, interpretation and summarisation cuts away at the value of the information
- **fortress mentality** – as businesses move from large centralised organisations to 'strategic' and autonomous business units with their own management boards the units become suspicious of head office, grow to love their autonomy and take steps to shield themselves from the prying eyes of head office by starving them of information. One of my own banking clients looked out of his boardroom window, just before a presentation I was due to make on corporate transformation and managing change, and sadly agreed that although the bank's competitor was a large US conglomerate the *enemy* was his business unit across the road
- **the dominance of statutory accountants** – if the accountants in the business focus on regulatory compliance, historic cost accounting, and accounting policies and practices to the exclusion of relevant management information and value-added advice, they can reduce the management to just looking at numbers. The leader's responsibility is to ensure that this is an assessment of *capability*, not a backward look at the existing situation.

A quantitative tool for unravelling some of this complexity is described below.

Activity Based Management Information

The term Activity Based Costing (ABC) was coined by Professor Kaplan of the Harvard Business School and H. Thomas Johnson in their book *Relevance Lost* (Harvard Business School Press, 1987). One of the main contentions was that traditional costing methods provided information too shackled by accounting policies and practices to be of value to the business. Professor Kaplan with Robin Cooper, a fellow professor, later proposed the ABC solution, which was quickly accepted by businesses in the US and UK. In the UK, Kaplan and Cooper in association with KPMG Management Consulting's Strategic Business Management Unit promoted ABC.

The key concepts of ABC, illustrated in Figure 7 below, are:

(1) activities consume resources
(2) cost drivers determine the nature of costs of activities
(3) products, brands, customers, market segments, regions or the business itself are the underlying reason for a 'pool' of activities.

ABC is simple and logical in that it asks the business, usually from cost centre manager to main board director, to answer some key and often threatening questions:

● What do you do (activities)
● How much does it cost (activity costing through cost attribution)
● How often do you do it (timing and frequency)
● Why do you do it and why this often (activity driver)
● What amount of work do you undertake in a given period (volume)
● Who or what benefits (activity object)?

Figure 7   *The key concepts of activity based costing*   **KPMG**

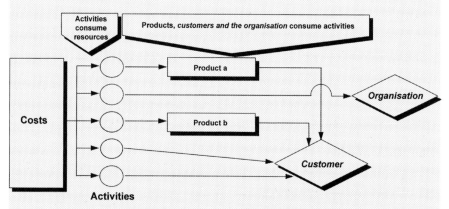

These basic concepts provide the means for cutting through the business complexity and
costing the activities and the products, customers and markets.

Activity Based Management (ABM) is a development of ABC that encompasses the various applications of activity based information in managing organisations. This is illustrated in Figure 8 below.

Figure 8   *Decision support – outsourcing*

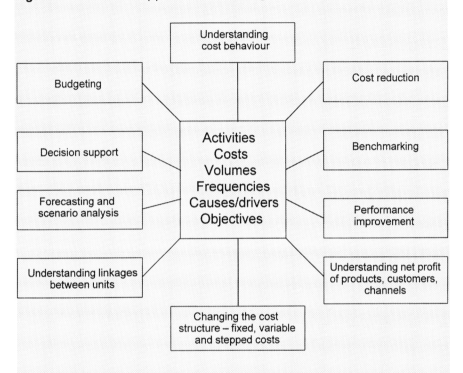

Example of use of ABM to support the outsourcing decision

In a major credit-card company ABM was applied across the group to determine if the transaction processing activities should be outsourced. The ABC techniques were used to calculate the cost of the activities across the group and identify a comprehensive specification of what was involved in processing in terms of activities, costs and volumes. From this informed position a number of companies were then invited to tender. At the end of the tendering process the company was able to discuss with each tenderer exactly what they would be getting for their money and to decide whether to outsource or set in train performance improvements to match the external best performer.

ABM has seriously challenged the conventional methods of costing and, more importantly, the role of financial information to support the business.

KNOW YOUR ENEMY

'... to cut my enemies to pieces, drive them before me, seize their possessions, witness the tears of those dear to them, and embrace their wives and daughters.'

Genghis Khan (aged 18)

Your second task is to understand your enemy's capabilities and limitations. A business must understand what drives its rivals. It is critical to know what motivates them, their commitment to their territory and what they are prepared to do to succeed.

A slightly looser interpretation of the term 'rival' will be used here by including suppliers as well as direct competitors. Suppliers will be seen in two roles. First, as those external agents who compete with a business for its profits, using their position power to take a share of the organisation's profits by bargaining with it on profit-determining factors such as price, delivery and product functionality. Secondly, as allies who create a profitable relationship with the business and share the market success.

Competitors

How easy competition would be if a business could know whatever it wanted to know about its competitors while they were denied such knowledge of the business. Unfortunately, such information is kept secret and its safeguard is protected by law. The procurement of such information would be illegal in most countries.

The following section examines what kinds of information a business would want to have and how such information could be procured in the absence of protective laws. In so doing, the potential consequences of such procurement methods and the alternative methods available will be examined.

Information required

When an organisation seeks to do business with a business with a different organisational or national identity, information on the relevant country, politics, legal environment, and market is, on its own, insufficient. The *softer information* regarding culture and values is critical to success. In dealing with a rival, whether a competitor, supplier or customer, it is important to understand the assumptions, mindset and ambitions of that rival. Today most organisations realise that they should see themselves from their customers' perspective. You must also ensure that your business sees itself from its rivals' perspective, that key people put themselves in the shoes of your rivals and adopt their viewpoint about the situation – how does it feel from the rival's side of the negotiating table?

Why did Britain fail to understand and manage the Pergau Dam episode better? The majority of the UK press felt very strongly that Britain had acted fairly and justly and that the evidence showed the Malaysians to be at fault. However, this judgement was based on the UK perspective which is fundamentally at odds with South-East Asian culture.

Hampden-Turner put forward a comparison of the alternate values which illustrate how fundamental misunderstandings occur and how they are inevitable. This is summarised below.

UK management	Oriental management
Legal-rational thinking	Relationship minded
Unambiguous communication	Ambiguous-suggestive communication
Inward-looking and self-interested	Communitarian
Separated egoism and altruism	Fused egoism and altruism
Rights, entitlement and personal prosperity	Obligations and communal achievement
Private gain and personal fulfilment	Group learning and natural development

Source: Hampden-Turner, 'Getting wiser about the Asians'
Director, June 1994

The two essential questions to predict what response a rival would make to an organisation's moves are:

(1)   What drives the rival?
(2)   What is the rival doing and what is he able to do?

Sun Tzu said: 'Thus, what enables the wise sovereign and the good general to strike and conquer, and achieve things beyond the reach of ordinary men, is foreknowledge.'

Michael Porter in *Competitive Strategy* (The Free Press, 1980) provides a simple competitor analysis framework, illustrated in Figure 9 below.

Figure 9   *The components of a competitor analysis*

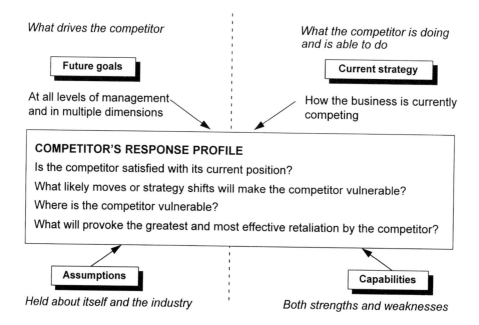

Adapted with the permission of The Free Press, a division of Simon & Schuster from COMPETITIVE STRATEGY: Techniques for Analyzing Industries and Competitors by Micahel E. Porter. Copyright © 1980 by The Free Press.

In a dynamic competitive situation the framework would need to be supplemented by real-time information on:

- the attack, defence or retaliation strategies adopted by the rivals and the success of these strategies
- their reactions to the organisation's moves
- the credibility of the public messages the rivals give and their response to the organisation's messages
- the actions the rivals intend to take and the products, services and strategies for promoting them.

Such competitor information is vital if a business is to move quickly and decisively against its rivals. Ensuring this happens is a CEO responsibility.

How to procure information

The accuracy of an organisation's prediction of its rivals' response is determined by the quality of the information it has to support the type of framework given in Figure 9. Hence Sun Tzu points to the importance of using spies, who can reduce the need for prediction by providing prior knowledge of all the elements in the framework.

Sun Tzu says that we should use spies 'of whom there are five classes: (1) local spies; (2) inward spies; (3) converted spies; (4) doomed spies; (5) surviving spies'. These are described below with recent examples that have tested the limits of legality.

Local spies

According to Sun Tzu, local spies live in the local region of the enemy. They provide information on the actions of the enemy in the locality and the perception of the local people. Such information provides an understanding of the enemy in its own territory.

The business equivalent is local agents, who, since they are not the employees of an organisation's rivals, can quite legitimately gather published and physical evidence of its activities.

Inward spies

Inward spies are the employees of an organisation's rivals. They provide a business with 'insider' information – private information not for public consumption. From 1993, an on-going battle raged between Volkswagen and General Motors based on whether Mr Jose Ignacio Lopez de Arriortua, former vice-president in charge of procurement at General Motors in Detroit, had stolen secret documents to assist the troubled Volkswagen group in attaining cost competitiveness.

A business can lure away the employees of its rivals by more lucrative employment contracts and set them to work utilising the knowledge, experience and skills gained with the rivals. Operating within the restrictions placed by employment contracts, this is common practice and is evident in merchant banking and securities trading where whole teams are often bought out from rivals.

Converted spies

According to Sun Tzu, converted spies are the spies employed by enemies that have been secretly converted to work as double agents. Since spies are held in some esteem and often by virtue of their position are able to surmise the intent of their masters, converted spies can provide knowledge of what drives the enemy, what the enemy is doing and is able to do. They also provide the opportunity to pass along information of no consequence.

The closest business application is the recruitment of information agencies or consultancies employed by rivals. Despite assurances of 'Chinese walls' within such organisations to segregate confidential information, the business is likely to benefit from the organisation's previous experience with and knowledge of the rival.

Doomed spies

According to Sun Tzu, doomed spies are used to provide misinformation. Having done so, other informants can denounce them as spies to the rivals. Hence they become doomed.

In business, the media are the best way of passing misinformation to rivals and are explored in some detail in Chapter Four.

Surviving spies

Surviving spies are the most secret and experienced of informants. They enter and bring back information from the rival's organisation. KAS, the intelligence firm of National Car Parks (NCP), deployed tactics including planting a former army captain as the personal assistant to the chairman of Europarks, surveillance of directors and checking dustbins and briefcases. The three-year surveillance was judged not to be illegal since it was not proven that NCP were trying to damage Europark's commercial interests.

Patrick Grayson of the London office of Kroll, the biggest commercial investigation group in the world, reported to the *Independent on Sunday* on 17 October 1993 in an article by David Bowen entitled 'Double agent in the office': 'We might ring up and say we are looking for such and such a product, and ask if the company is manufacturing it. Or I might say I am a potential supplier, and ask about plans for the future.' He goes on to describe how using 'a bit of subterfuge', an investigator posing as a supplier, a customer or perhaps a technical journalist could get on to a factory tour. The purpose of the tour was to examine whether a rival group had the same process as their client. As Mr Grayson points out in the article: 'In business there is no such thing as fair – there is legal and ethical, but fair and unfair aren't terms that can be used'.

Remote spies

With the advent of computer technology, it may be desirable to add a new category, the remote spy. British Airways staff, for example, were caught hacking into the computers of its competitor, Virgin Atlantic, to try to lure away passengers with better offers. Despite an out-of-court settlement the battle for compensation continued.

In most cases, what a business wants to know about its competitors can be easily acquired through a thorough review of published material: newspapers, articles, brokers' reports, press releases and independent industry analysts and reporters.

Suppliers

It is important to recognise that the supplier relationship will always have some healthy tension in it to ensure that each organisation acts to satisfy their stakeholders. Towards which end of the spectrum ranging from partnership to rivalry do your suppliers lie? Collect some simple information of the type below from your procurement department and make a quick assessment of whether your current major suppliers are your allies or your rivals.

Are your suppliers partners or rivals?

- Do you regularly discuss the state of the market and what that may mean for your demand for the suppliers' products?
- Do you have common and easy ways of exchanging information, for example electronic orders and invoices?
- Do you supply forecasts of demand, updated as soon as the situation changes?
- Do the suppliers understand your business and especially how their product gets used in your process?
- Do they tell you how best you can use their products in your business?
- Do both of you jointly make investments and changes to your processes and technologies to ensure that the overall efficiency is enhanced?
- Do you understand each other's profit from the transaction?
- Do both of you tell each other what your rivals are buying and selling at?

If you answered 'no' more often than 'yes', your relationship is not a partnership.

In *Competitive Strategy* Michael Porter highlights the need to select suppliers such that the best bargaining position can be created. The key information requirements in assessing whether a business is in a more powerful bargaining position are given below. If the answers to the following questions are largely 'yes' business is likely to be dominant:

- Do a large number of suppliers exist and is the business in an industry with fewer (less concentration of) buyers
- Do substitute products or services exist for the products or services suppliers offer
- Does the industry represent a significant percentage of the suppliers' sales, thereby making the business an important customer
- Do the suppliers provide products or services that are relatively unimportant inputs to the business
- Does the supplier provide an undifferentiated product at low cost thus making the switching of demand between suppliers easy
- Are there effective barriers to the supplier entering the organisation's market?

If the business can gather information to address these questions it can make a judgement as to its relative bargaining positions. Although the result of Porter's analysis is not necessarily hostility between supplier and buyer, a strongly dominant position can change the balance of power and therefore profit.

Power in the food industry lies increasingly in the hands of the retailer. Recent events indicate how the supermarket chains have used this to agree terms with the manufacturer. This, combined with considerations of efficiency and effectiveness in the management of the supply chain, have resulted in retailers dictating:

- the times when deliveries are to be made to retailer depots
- the passing of electronic and telephone orders
- the specification of product size for shelf-stocking, storing and transportation
- the promotion of products, for example Sainsbury's telling Cadbury's that it would like to see its chocolate packaging say '15 pence off the next purchase'.

In *Competitive Advantage* Porter points to a need to examine the **value system** within an industry. The value system provides a potentially collaborative strategy between successive buyers and suppliers in the supply chain, from extractors of materials to the front-end suppliers of product and service to end consumers. This is illustrated by example in Figure 10 below which uses the chemical industry value system.

Figure 10   *Chemical industry value system*

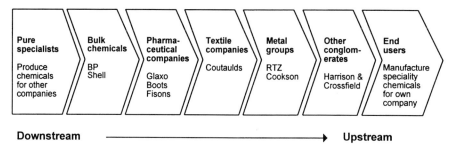

Downstream ───────────────────────────→ Upstream

A business needs to gather information about suppliers that helps it to understand its bargaining position and decide whether it would be more profitable to compete or collaborate with them. The factors that lead to **collaborative strategies in the value system** are:

- economies of integration, such as economies in the production process, in the size of management overhead, in the amount of downstream and upstream market information, through avoiding upstream selling and marketing
- linking and tapping into each other's technology and information systems
- certainty of supply and demand enabling just in time processes to be implemented
- offsetting bargaining power
- creating an enhanced ability to differentiate by a more integrated approach to the market place between manufacturers, distributors and retailers
- potential for increasing entry barriers

- making a higher return by entering a high-return downstream or upstream business
- defending, or creating relationships which prohibit rivals from sources of supply or demand.

These factors are explored in depth by Porter in *Competitive Strategy*. The **information requirements** to support such value-system strategies are extensive and include:

- an understanding of the costs, performance and profits of each value point in the total value system
- an understanding of the players, their size, profitability and bargaining power at each juncture in the value system
- the part played by technology in the value system and the dependency of the players in information for their ability to act
- the avoidable costs and enhanced profits if a business grouped parts of the chain together
- the threats to the profitability of the industry that could be avoided
- the impact on rivals of relationships between the business and various suppliers, customers and rivals.

Such information can be gathered and modelled largely from publicly available information and from information gathered from front-line staff – procurement, sales, service and maintenance. Marks & Spencer is an excellent example of a company that truly understands the strength of its position, its suppliers and customers and which utilises this information and its power to control the value system.

It can be seen that the line between friend and foe is indeed a fine one and depends very much on the choices made between collaboration or conflict. This theme will be discussed again in relation to determining positional response.

Marks & Spencer, the premier UK clothing and food retailer, has made supplier–retailer relationship management an art and a science. M&S has the foremost quality and value image in the mind of the consumer. It also has the record for the greatest sales per square foot over a number of years through its flagship London store, Marble Arch, Oxford Street. M&S has a network of suppliers that it has nurtured over a number of years by taking a large percentage of total output specified to its standards, advising on sourcing, production process and policy on sale or return. In the 1980s move to high fashion across M&S stores, M&S suppliers found themselves having to introduce flexible manufacturing to take into account changes in colour and cut, smaller batch sizes and lower margins whilst maintaining quality if they were not to suffer from the famous M&S 'no-fuss' goods return policy.

KNOW YOUR POSITION

To understand its position, a business needs to combine the macro-environmental information with knowledge of its industry, its markets and customers. Over the last decade, Michael Porter has transformed the way that businesses think about industry-level information. His 'industry structure analysis' has become a standard way of understanding the attractiveness of the industry and the basic attractiveness of an organisation's position within it.

Your third task is to understand your position: where has your industry ended up as a result of the multitude of decisions taken by all those having a say – customers, suppliers, rivals, regulators? The following section quickly runs through some of the core analysis that can help you appreciate your position.

Industry structure analysis

Using the framework in Figure 11 below the key elements of the macro-level information can be utilised to determine their impact on the structure of an industry and its resulting attractiveness, ie its profit potential. The factors determining industry structure affect the profit, cost and investment requirements for those choosing to compete in the market.

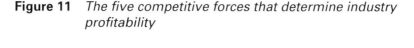

Figure 11   *The five competitive forces that determine industry profitability*

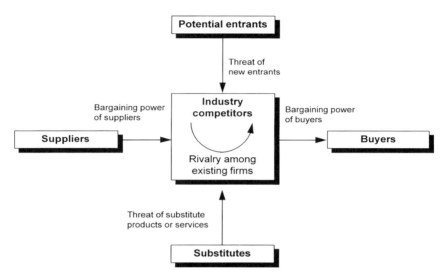

In assessing its position within the industry and the profit potential, costs and investment requirements, the key information needed is:

- **the extent of barriers to entry** – if entry barriers are low, more competitors will be able to enter the industry and partake of the market share and profits of the industry
- **the power of buyers** – if the power of buyers is high then the profits of suppliers will be low
- **the power of suppliers** – if the power of suppliers is high then the prices they charge will be high at the expense of buyers
- **the availability of substitutes** – if substitutes are available for the products of the industry then the profits of the suppliers will be limited because buyers will always have the choice of going elsewhere
- **the intensity of rivalry** – if the intensity of rivalry is high then the competitors will by competition erode the extra profits available in the industry and may continue to compete with very low margins.

Such an assessment enables you to determine whether and how to enhance your position or to withdraw from the fray.

Following on from the example of the chemical industry value system, the application of the framework is illustrated in Figure 12 below using a simple example from the UK do-it-yourself/home improvement industry.

Figure 12 *Illustration from the UK DIY market*

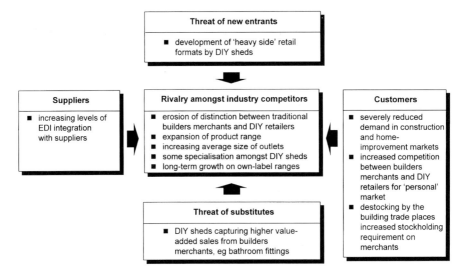

Having understood the industry context, a business needs to examine the specific area in which it competes in more detail. This requires an understanding of the markets and customers that populate the area of the industry that the business is covering.

Market segmentation

In getting to know the customer and market a key technique for analysis is market segmentation. This is the identification of the potentially unique needs and wants within the overall market. Each individual has a set of particular requirements and to create the best fit between an organisation's offerings and the individual requires a unique and perfectly tailored proposition to be made.

Perfect tailoring is obviously an uneconomic situation for all but the large project-based companies that sell a few high-value projects. However, to manage its position better a business can segment the customer needs into groups of potential buyers who possess similar characteristics. The bases of segmentation and hence the information requirements are as follows:

- **demographics**, ie by age, sex, family size, race, religion, ethnic origin, education, profession
- **geographic**, ie by location – countries, states, regions, cities, localities
- **socio-cultural and lifestyle**, ie by social class, lifestyle, values
- **economic**, ie by income and expenditure group
- **consumption pattern**, ie by usage rate, occasion, impulse, loyalty.

Segmentation and the mapping of existing coverage of each segment can point to the gaps in satisfaction of customer needs.

The key information requirements to support these strategies are based on the characteristics of the market and the segments that populate it. Table 3 below illustrates ways of structuring such information and how the different bases of segmentation point to different opportunities.

Table 3 *Market segmentation debt information (percentages)*

	Sex		Age					Socio-economic group				Region			
	Male	Female	16–24	25–34	35–44	45–64	65+	AB	C1	C2	DE	South	Midlands/ Wales	North/ Scotland	Total
Overdraft	16	8	14	19	18	8	2	13	17	12	6	15	10	10	12
Personal loans	14	8	12	18	19	6	1	10	15	14	5	9	13	12	11
Loans from friends/relatives	4	2	7	4	3	1	0	1	7	2	2	4	2	3	3
Mortgages	34	33	10	53	61	40	4	42	46	37	15	34	35	31	33
Credit cards	24	20	14	29	35	23	8	31	28	20	12	26	17	20	21
Store cards	6	6	4	9	10	5	1	6	7	6	4	5	6	7	6
Hire purchase	7	5	5	12	8	5	6	5	4	9	6	6	5	7	6
Catalogues	9	19	14	22	22	12	2	6	9	14	23	9	15	19	14
Finance house/ leasing	1	0	0	2	2	0	0	0	1	1	1	1	0	1	1
Pawnbroker	0	0	0	0	0	0	0	0	0	0	0	0	0	0	0
Money lender	0	0	0	0	1	0	0	0	0	0	1	1	0	0	0
Other	1	0	1	2	1	1	0	1	1	1	1	1	1	0	1
None	40	43	46	24	15	39	85	37	33	38	56	42	42	42	42

Source: Social Surveys (Gallup Polls) Ltd/Key Note, April 1992

Figure 13 *Market segment debt analysis*

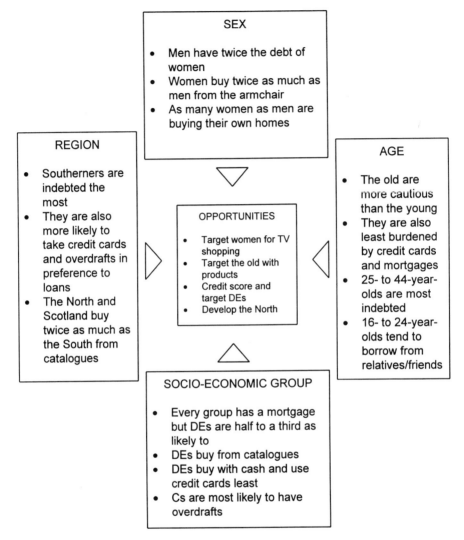

The combined segmentation analysis in Table 3 allows some broader judgements about the behaviour of the population to be formed, for example:

- pensioners are not burdened by debt
- men aged 25 to 44, living in the south and working in skilled manual jobs, are most in debt
- 42% of the total have no debt whatsoever
- one-third are burdened by mortgages
- one-fifth have at least one credit card

- 12% have an overdraft
- 11% have personal loans
- 6% have store cards or hire-purchase debt.

An analysis within each basis of segmentation reveals some interesting information and opportunities as shown in Figure 13 above. Information regarding customer actions, if well structured, can help a business to understand customer preferences better and help it to identify opportunities. Traditional segmentation of the market will help you to understand your customers. Your challenge is to ensure you segment customer needs in a way that allows you to identify unsatisfied needs and ones that customers have only dreamed about. The technique of segmentation can be used more creatively by segmenting customers along lines such as:

- lifestyle – how customers spend their time
- dreams – what they may subconsciously want
- values – what set of beliefs they subscribe to
- self-image – how they see themselves
- ambitions – what they want to be.

In the highly competitive UK premium ice-cream market, Häagen-Daz's ice cream managed to capture 32.3% market share in 1993. The next in position were New England, and Thornton and Loseley; new entrants include Vermont, USA's Ben & Jerry's ice cream and Italy's Ranieri brand which was introduced by Wall's. The market niche these companies target appears to be the same. So how can a new entrant establish itself? The answer perhaps lies in the information communicated to the customer and whether this can be better allied to the customer's value set. The table below illustrates the potential messages that Ben & Jerry's or Ranieri could give.

Häagen-Daz's values	Alternative values (1)	Alternative values (2)
Empathy	Fun	Balance
Hedonism	Eccentricity	Individualism
Androgeny	Adventurousness	Empathy
		Creativity
		Aesthetics

DETERMINE YOUR POSITIONAL RESPONSE

Information of the type described above will help you to understand yourself, your rival and your position. Your challenge is to ensure that your people work to identify advantageous positions within the value system and also seek to identify new positions as yet unimagined by rivals and customers.

You should begin by looking at the broad competitive positions available. You should then look at the impact of industry maturity and life cycle on your position. Next you should look at your options based on the characteristics of the market terrain itself. Finally, you should challenge the mindset of your people to seek out uncharted positions.

Broad competitive positions

The previous three steps illustrate that a business has a choice between competition and collaboration. Suppliers can be an integral part of a business if it chooses to bring them into the organisation through sharing plans, systems, managers, knowledge, ventures and, ultimately, profits. Competitors can also become allies if businesses 'collude' to safeguard the profitability of their industry by erecting entry barriers against new rivals, sharing innovation, adopting compatible pricing strategies, striking joint ventures in some areas, giving advance warnings of their moves and, ultimately, sharing the profits in the industry. However, such measures can become hallowed by the passage of time and make the business vulnerable to a new entrant who is prepared to break the 'rules' that have been tacitly created. Therefore, collaboration and the need to safeguard industry profitability must be balanced against the need to maintain competitive innovation and lightness of foot in seizing opportunities.

Michael Porter highlights three **generic** competitive strategies (illustrated in Figure 14 below) in which four **competitive** strategies are allowed:

- market to all segments industry-wide with a cross-segment product or service competing on the basis of differentiation
- market to all segments industry-wide with a cross-segment product or service competing on the basis of overall cost leaders
- target a particular segment with a product or service focused to compete on the bases of differentiation
- target a particular segment with a product or service focused to compete on the bases of cost leadership

Figure 14 *Three generic strategies*

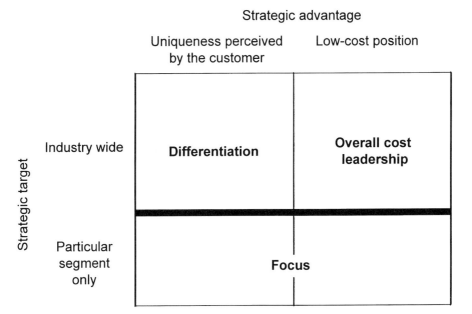

Strategic advantage

Uniqueness perceived   Low-cost position
by the customer

Industry wide	**Differentiation**	**Overall cost leadership**
Particular segment only		**Focus**

Strategic target

Adapted with the permission of The Free Press, a division of Simon & Schuster from COMPETITIVE STRATEGY: Techniques for Analyzing Industries and Competitors by Micahel E. Porter. Copyright © 1980 by The Free Press.

Industry situations – maturity, life cycle and terrain

These positioning strategies are the basis of deciding actions in relation to the maturity, life cycle and **structure** of the industry. Porter then examines how these can be translated into actions dependent upon the particular industry **situation**.

The characteristics of various industry situations and the competitive strategies and tactics that can be adopted are given in Table 4 below.

Table 4   *Competitive strategies and tactics by industry type*

Industry type	Characteristics of industry situation (examples)	Competitive strategies and tactics (examples)	Information requirements
Fragmented, ie no company has a strong market share and can strongly influence the industry outcome	• low overall entry barriers • high transportation costs • no great size economies • diverse market needs • exit barriers	• create well-managed, minimum-cost small units • increase the value added • specialise by product, customer type, geography, 'basics' products	• How many players are there in the market? • What are the market shares of each player?
Emerging, ie newly formed or re-created industries created by innovation, new customer needs or other macro-level changes	• technological or strategic uncertainty • small production volume • newly formed companies • first-time buyers • very high short-term demand	Set the 'rules of the game', ie: • pricing • marketing, products • develop the industry or pursue self-advancement with great speed • strike early agreements with suppliers and channels • exploit first-mover advantages	• How long have the current products been in existence? • How long have the current players been in the market? • What is the rate of new-product introduction? • How big is the market and is it growing fast?
Mature, ie a state where industry growth has flattened	• increased rivalry for share based on cost and service • slow-down in capacity addition • no/few new products • entry of new international rivals • increases in strength of channels	• focus on one generic strategy • rationalise the product range • price the product line • redesign processes • sell to existing customers better • buy assets sold by exiting rivals • sell to profitable customers, regions • sell in other markets	• Has growth ceased but not yet declined? • Have the market players been in the market for many years? • Is price competition resulting? • Has new-product introduction ceased?
Declining, ie a state where industry growth has permanently declined	• declining and uncertain demand • exit barriers • volatility of rivalry	• seek leadership • create or defend a niche • exit slowly, maximising cash flows during the exit • exit as soon as possible	• Is the market growth and size declining? • Are players leaving the market?

Industry type	Characteristics of industry situation (examples)	Competitive strategies and tactics (examples)	Information requirements
Global, ie the position of rivals in major geographic or national markets is fundamentally affected by their overall global positions	• technological advances increasing economies • decreased transportation costs • reduced government constraints • emergence of common demands across countries	• compete on the full product range worldwide • sell to a particular segment worldwide • focus on satisfying national differences • exploit government barriers to entry	• What percentage of sales are by global players? • Are cross-national sales important? • Are companies sourcing materials internationally? • Is the same product sold inter-nationally?

A radically different way of examining position is presented by Sun Tzu. This is based on the structural characteristics of the terrain, which equates in business to the resulting market itself, ie the outcome of the industry structural forces that Michael Porter describes. Both propositions, Sun Tzu's and Porter's, are valid. However, Sun Tzu's advice is aimed primarily at providing guidelines for situational tactical responses, whilst Porter's is aimed at providing a framework for strategy formulation.

Table 5 below describes Sun Tzu's military and competitive tactics arising from position as derived from *The Art of War*.

Table 5 *Sun Tzu's military and competitive tactics*

Types of terrain	Information required to determine the characteristics of equivalent market situations	Military tactics	Competitive tactics	Information you should collect to help determine your tactics (example)
Accessible ground, ie ground which can be freely traversed by yourself and the enemy	• low entry and exit barriers	• occupy the best spots before the enemy and guard lines of supply	• move first to enter • create an advantageous supply chain, tying up channels if possible	• Are rivals already present or planning entry? • Are channels available?

Types of terrain	Information required to determine the characteristics of equivalent market situations	Military tactics	Competitive tactics	Information you should collect to help determine your tactics (example)
Entangling ground, ie ground which can be abandoned easily but is hard to re-occupy	• low exit barriers but high re-entry barriers, amounting to high switching costs, eg because existing players will buy your capacity but will fight re-entry	• if the enemy is unprepared he can be defeated • if prepared and you fail to defeat him then, return being impossible, disaster will ensue	• leave such a market with care • if you decide to re-enter such a market, you need to be sure that you have the resources and strategy to win	• Is this market of longer-term/strategic value to you? • Are rivals planning to occupy this territory? • If so, what will be the damage to you?
Temporising ground, ie ground from which neither side will gain from making the first move	• low first-mover advantages	• the enemy's bait should not be taken • you should retreat, thus enticing the enemy to pursue you, and then attack	• you should make the noises that will encourage others to move first • it would be better to let your rivals invest in inventing the products for the market and for you to copy and improve on their results	• Who can you entice to enter first? • Are there ways of making entry into this market easier, eg joint venture?
Narrow passes: the strategic rule is that these should be occupied first to await the coming of the enemy	• high first-mover advantages based on focused dominance of a niche	• if you occupy them first, you should garrison them strongly and await the enemy • if the enemy is first, you should not follow unless the enemy's garrison is weak	• new market niches should be entered first • strong entry barriers should be built up • existing niches should only be entered if the existing players' positions are weak in terms of satisfying customer demands	• What are the means available to restrict competition for the best niches? • Which niches held by rivals must be attacked to secure longer-term positions?

Types of terrain	Information required to determine the characteristics of equivalent market situations	Military tactics	Competitive tactics	Information you should collect to help determine your tactics (example)
Precipitous heights: The strategic rule is that these should also be occupied first to await the coming of the enemy	• high first-mover advantages based on gaining an overall dominant position	• occupy the best spots and wait for the enemy to come up • once in such a dominant position your actions cannot be dictated by the enemy	• a strong overall position should be built up with speed to enable you to exploit the position against all rivals	• What are the key positions that you should invest in and make impregnable?
Positions at a great distance from the enemy	Positions outside the mainstream strategy of your rivals, probably involving: • entering new markets with existing products, or • new products for existing markets. These strategies or tactics are called alternately avoidance, bypass or differentiation	• if the enemy has occupied such positions then you should retreat and try to entice him away • if you are situated thus, then whether you provoke a battle or not will depend on your relative size	• if attractive new markets are occupied by your rivals then you should attack them in established markets where they have a lot to lose and thereby divert their attention • if you are established in lucrative new markets you may use these funds to attack your rivals in established markets only if you have better overall resources than them	• Which of your rivals' positions are most vulnerable to attack and which would cause them to lose their expansion focus? • What product-market gaps exist that you can easily fill without soliciting attack?

Extensive data is needed to enable a business to successfully pursue territorial strategies and tactics is extensive and real-time information is required to assess moves and countermoves. In summary, the **key information** to support such strategies and tactics is:

- sufficient information regarding the **market** to identify which of Sun Tzu's six types of market situations the business is facing or which market situations would be favourable to the business if it could steer its rivals into them
- information regarding the position of **rivals**, largely focusing on their size, for which the business can use market share data, and security of position, for which the business needs to assess the extent to which the rivals satisfy customer requirements
- monitoring of emerging **technologies** and needs relevant to the markets within which the business competes to understand the potential they offer to its current position or to creating new positions
- identification of **opportunities to create new positions** by exploiting business strengths in existing markets or products
- identification of **opportunities to differentiate and** accumulate funds to enable the business **to reinforce** its position or attack its rival's position.

Tables 4 and 5 illustrate the positions the business should adopt based on the overall industry situation it is facing and the dynamics of the environment. But what are the operational choices available to create competitive advantages? Porter points to a range of choices the business has in creating its position, as illustrated in Figure 15 below.

The factors in Figure 15 drive how a business is positioned and how it can reposition. For example the business can:

- consolidate production units to gain economies of scale
- link distribution channels to better push its full range of products
- work production machinery 24 hours per day to better utilise capacity
- take-over suppliers of key components to secure control over the technology and secure supply and quality of inputs

- ensure that business units exchange best practice in sales and marketing
- speed up the time to market for new products
- relocate its back office in a country with lower costs and better infrastructure
- introduce human resources and remuneration policies to encourage performance-related incentives
- lobby government for licences for home-grown products and fight to restrict entry by overseas rivals.

Such factors will determine the strength and assailability of the organisation's operational position.

Figure 15 *Operational choices of creating competitive advantage*

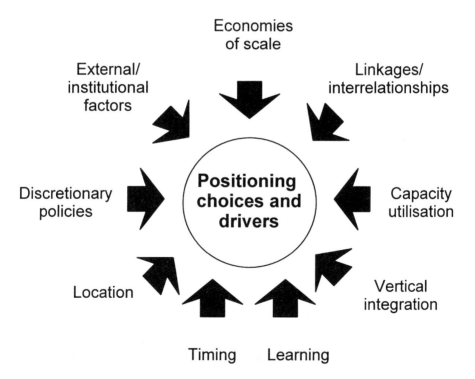

Compete for uncharted territories

Your responsibility as leader is not just to conquer existing territories. Although this is vital, you must also lead the organisation to new discoveries. This requires you to be a pioneer and explorer. Exploration demands questioning and unconventional minds, an acceptance of uncertainty while managing the risk of failure, perseverance in the face of scepticism and setbacks, and sharing rewards. In the discovery of new territories, much of the position analysis described in this chapter will not help you. Some will only be of value once you have arrived to help you decide on the best position for your business.

To create new territories your company must answer the following questions:

- Who are the customers of the future?
- What will be their desires, ambitions and needs?
- What are the potential range of benefits you must supply to satisfy their needs?
- What competencies are required to deliver these benefits?

The answer to these questions will come from developing insight and foresight into:

- industry trends
- technology levers and developments
- changes in related industries
- lessons from changes in unconnected industries with similar characteristics
- people's (potential buyers') aspirations and frustrations.

The leaders in positioning for uncharted territories will be those who have intellectual leadership not just financial strength, vivid imaginations not just excellent customer service, stamina for the long haul not just short-term returns.

*IN THIS CHAPTER*_____

We have examined how a business can come to know itself a little better and what it would want to know about its rivals. Lessons from Sun Tzu pointing to the importance of 'insider' information have been interpreted in the context of legal, modern-day information acquisition. It was found that the limits of ethical if not legal behaviour in acquiring intimate relevant information are already being tested. In the context of what a business knows about itself, we also examined its rivals and suppliers, the decision as to whether to compete or collaborate.

Based on an understanding of the business and its enemies, position was examined. With the help of Michael Porter the type of industry surrounding the business was identified and thereby the types of strategic choices available. Then, with the help of Sun Tzu, the terrain immediately surrounding the business was examined and the tactics available to advance or retreat from its position were identified. Finally, the information needed to support such strategies and tactics was identified. The principles of the chapter are summarised in Figure 16 below.

Your leadership challenge is to ensure your organisation adopts competitively advantageous positions and systematically seeks out new and uncharted competitive territories in which it can reap the benefits of moving in first.

The next chapter goes on to examine position from the point of view of formulating and implementing responses. In so doing the discussion moves from strategy to action and counter-action.

Figure 16   *Determining position: know yourself, your enemy and your position*

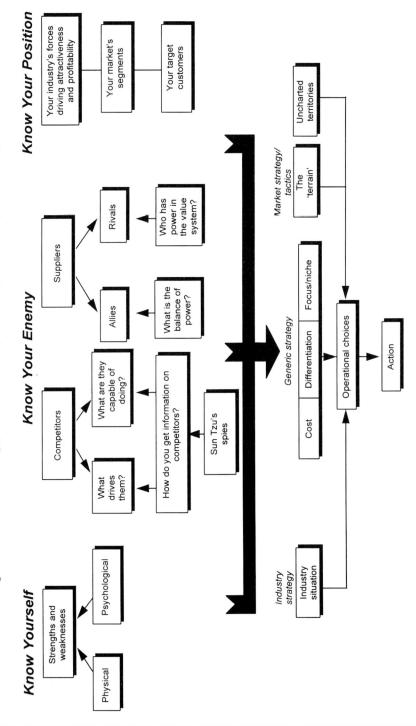

LEADERSHIP CHALLENGE
FOUR

*Ensure you pick fights that you can win
and win the fights that you pick*

Chapter Four

RESPONDING: ATTACK, DEFENCE AND RETALIATORY STRATEGIES

'*In my strategy, the training for killing enemies is by way of many contests, fighting for survival, discovering the meaning of life and death, learning the Way of the sword, judging the strength of attacks and understanding the Way of the "edge and ridge" of the sword.*'

Miyamoto Musashi (1645)

INTRODUCTION

As Musashi points out, the best way of learning the strategy of attack, defence and retaliation is through practice. It is not desirable to be so preoccupied with the theory of strategy and planning as to lose sight of its practice. The intellectual exercise will take up precious time whilst the business is being attacked, its own attacks are being defended and retaliation is undermining its position. How long does your annual strategy, planning and budgeting round take: half a year, a quarter, a month or so? Probably closer to the half year than you would like to admit. If only a powerful planning machine could be created which could quickly explore and explain the implications of the organisation's strategies and those of its rivals.

This chapter will look at the principles of strategy formulation and the execution of attack, defence and retaliatory strategies. We will begin by taking a look at the role that you, the leader, must play to meet the challenge. The lesson in unbeatable attack, defence and retaliation comes from Genghis Khan.

MEETING CHALLENGE FOUR

To meet the leadership challenge you must demonstrate the ability to attack, defend and retaliate effectively. The key leadership quality to meet this challenge is **relationship management**, which requires:

- game planning and playing
- toughness in action and thought
- the ability to shape people's expectations, and
- energy and endurance to last the course of what could be a lengthy series of parries and cross-parries.

Other key leadership qualities you will need to support you are:

- visualisation of the potential outcomes
- clear, fast, broad and evolving neural processes, and
- a deep sense of belief and destiny.

Leadership entails significant responsibilities. These include ensuring that:

- information is gathered on your rivals and processed to determine *what* to attack
- similar information is gathered to predict your rivals' likely first strikes and retaliations in order to prepare your organisation's defence
- the organisation is prepared for swift and effective retaliation
- resources are available to fulfil attack, defence and retaliation strategies.

If you cannot discharge this responsibility you will lead your organisation to competitive defeat.

GENGHIS KHAN (1167–1227)

Born Temujin, the son of a Mongol chieftan, Genghis Khan grew up in a tough and highly competitive world. At the age of 12 his father was poisoned by Tartars and he and his family were abandoned by their tribe. They fled and were pursued by the father's enemies for years. In time, he fought for and gained power. At 25 Genghis Khan had defeated all but two rival tribes. He attacked the more powerful of the two when his spies reported his enemy's unpreparedness. Following 3 days of slaughter he prevailed and immediately went on to defeat the remaining opposition. In 1202, he exacted a terrible vengeance from the Tartars for the murder of his father. Having defeated them, he had every male prisoner taller than the centre of a cartwheel slaughtered. Three years later, he had all except a few of the remaining Tartars exterminated. In 1206, he was proclaimed Genghis Khan, leader of all the Mongols.

Genghis Khan proceeded to create a professional army out of the tough herders, hunters, horse traders, petty bandits and mercenaries that comprised his people. He believed in a clear chain of command and organised his army into tens. A troop consisted of ten men. Ten troops made a squadron. Ten squadrons made a regiment. Ten regiments made a division. Finally, two or more divisions made an army. Genhis Khan's personal bodyguard was also the special reserve from which officers were selected and comprised 10,000 men. He trained his army for flexibility and mobility and enforced strict discipline. He introduced a constitution called the Yasaq. Non-compliance meant death. The basic assumption was that he had divine right to rule and punish.

Genghis Khan's strategy was applied on a grand scale. Each campaign was planned meticulously, taking into consideration the enemy, the resources, the landscape, supplies and communications. Of critical importance was the use of intelligence. He utilised a wide range of agents to procure information: merchants, discontented groups, spies and traitors. When he attacked, it was rapidly, with his armies spread wide in a broad fan. This strategy magnified his strength, terrified the enemy and left them unable to assess which army to attack. Couriers rode fast along the front to pass instructions and collect information. This structure enabled him to encircle his enemy and annihilate them. Defeated enemies were pursued and slaughtered. Mercy was forbidden without express authority from Genghis Khan himself.

Genghis Khan had his eyes on China and quickly conquered the Chinese province of Hsi-Hsia. He then crossed the Great Wall of China and lay siege to the walled cities. By 1215, he had captured the capital, Beijing. He was just over 40 when he acquired the title of Great Khan. In the 1220s, his armies had begun to attack the well-defended Russian cities. By 1223, his Mongol force had defeated two Russian armies. When he died at the age of 60, his empire and vassal kingdoms ranged from Persia to Outer Mongolia, Siberia, and south and east of China to Tibet and Korea.

Emissaries from Europe who had visited Genghis Khan's court reported that amongst themselves the Mongols were obedient, generous and honest. The in-fighting of the pre-Khan era had been eradicated through the enforcement of the Yasaq. All peoples inside the Mongol frontiers were treated with rough justice. To his people, Genghis Khan was a wise and just leader. Several of his lieutenants were brave enemies who had submitted. He had the genius, ruthless will and methods to make a professional army out of barbarians.

Genghis Khan left a working dynasty split amongst his four sons, one of whom was the famous Kublai Khan. To the outside world the Khan was no doubt the 'accursed', a cruel, merciless and vengeful terroriser. The lessons to be learned come from his astounding ability to attack and defend and his uncompromising ability to retaliate.

PRINCIPLES OF STRATEGY

'*The whole art of war consists in a well-reasoned and extremely circumspect defensive, followed by rapid and audacious attack.*'

Napoleon

J.R. Elting in *The Superstrategists* (WH Allen, 1987) summarises the relevant principles in formulating winning military strategies. We will take each of these in turn and demonstrate how companies have acted on these principles to win in corporate competitive situations. Then a checklist will be provided of the information needed to execute attack, defence and retaliatory strategies. Your challenge is to ensure that your organisation attacks, defends and retaliates with a determination to win.

Objective

'*... to achieve a decisive, obtainable result ... Just as the armed forces' objective must support the achievement of the overall national objective, so must the objectives of subordinate military forces contribute directly to attainment of the major military objective.*'

Key information or assessment:

- statement of mission, vision or intent followed by key objectives for realising the mission
- sub-objectives articulated by divisions, functions, subsidiaries, etc congruent with the key objectives.

Komatsu, the major Japanese manufacturer and supplier of earth-moving equipment, in its now-famous and well-documented battle against its mammoth rival Caterpillar, declared its objective to all its employees to 'encircle Caterpillar'. It proceeded on a strategy to match and, in some cases, beat Caterpillar in almost every market in terms of product, price and service.

Offensive

'*... seize, keep and exploit the initiative ... Victory requires offensive action, carrying the war to the enemy and into his own territories.*'

Key information or assessment:

- the specific areas to attack that will yield success
- the capability of the rival to retaliate and his speed of response.

In 1990, a retail revolution was gaining ground due to US pressures to open up markets. The expected benefits were greater consumer choice, efficiency gains in distribution network and intense competition resulting in price and value benefits to the consumer.

Toys 'R' Us, Japan, seized, kept and exploited the initiative begun by the US Government to open up the Japanese toy market. It caused a furore among toy-shop owners in the city of Niigata when it announced its plan to target the 500,000 population with its products and announced plans to build 15,000 square metres of shopping space over 3 years. The toy industry was worth $5.5bn in Japan. Toys 'R' Us set the pace in the fight for this market by announcing it expected to get 50% of the toy market in Niigata city and that it would build 100 stores over 10 years by providing consumers with what they wanted: high-quality, designer-branded labels.

Source: 'Western firms jostle for a share in Japan's retail revolution', *Multinational Business*, no 3, 1990

Unity of command

'*The forces engaged in any military operation must be under one responsible commander who has full authority over his subordinate commanders and their subordinates.*'

Key information or assessment:

- clear information on the command and control structure and the delegated levels of authority for implementing the objective.

Without unity of command, resources are wasted and divided. Alexander the Great provides a powerful and innovative example of unity of command in a takeover situation.

In his war against Darius, the Persian king, Alexander had routed his enemy twice and his policy of liberating the provinces occupied by Darius had allowed him to advance with his army largely intact. However, Alexander was soon faced with the problem of needing to advance whilst leaving behind him native populations loyal to Darius. If he could not solve this problem he would be forced to leave behind strong garrisons and turn from being liberator to occupier.

Alexander's solution was simple and effective. He could not immediately win over the people so he decided to win over the leaders. He began by identifying leaders who respected his prowess more than that of Darius. Alexander asked them to appoint him their king and then allowed them to retain their power and authority. Thus a policy of liberation was replaced by a policy of partnership that aligned objectives. Soon other leaders followed suit. This position was safeguarded by retaining military control in the hands of his Macedonians.

Put simplistically, in corporate terms, unity of command is created by keeping loyal and competent existing management in charge of their businesses following a takeover, while retaining control over their purse strings and thus their investment strategy.

Mass

'*The fundamental law of military strategy is: be stronger than your enemy at the decisive time and place.*'

Key information or assessment:

- the points to attack that will yield the greatest chance of success – this requires knowledge of the critical success factors and the rival's strengths and weaknesses on each factor.

The Swiss watch industry had built an international reputation for quality, precision jewellery. Timex attacked this pre-eminent position by manufacturing affordable and cheap watches and sold them in every market through chemists, supermarkets, and electrical shops as well as jewellers. This allowed it to launch its attack in a way that prevented its Swiss rivals from retaliating. A like-for-like attack on Timex would have undermined existing Swiss products and retail outlets and played to the strengths of Timex.

Economy of force

'*. . . concentrate the necessary combat power for decisive offensives.*'

Key information or assessment:

- the minimum resources required for success in the primary and secondary areas of importance.

Hewlett Packard in 1981 had the ambition of competing against the giants in the computer industry on their own ground. It soon became obvious that this would not work – HP could not beat IBM on the larger machines. HP focused its attention on a few niches whilst maintaining a strong, highly innovative but small position in other markets. Its presence in printers paid off and made it the benchmark manufacturer in that segment in the space of a few years.

Manoeuvre

'*. . . is the art of moving combat power by land, water, air and/or space . . . it is the means of attaining mass, the offensive, surprise and economy of force.*'

Key information or assessment:

- knowledge of rival's position
- knowledge of the terrain – for which read the market place
- knowledge of the means of mobilising/transporting resources.

Lieutenant General Pagonis ran the logistics for the Persian Gulf War campaign of 1992. His organisation's numbers grew from 5000 to 40,000. This team provided food, clothes, shelter and arms to 550,000 people; they served 122 million meals; they transported and distributed over 7 million tons of supplies, 117,000 vehicles and 2,000 helicopters, providing 1.3 billion gallons of fuel. This was all achieved over a few months to support a military strategy in a harsh environment with no previous infrastructure.

Source: William G. Pagonis, 'The work of the leader' *Harvard Business Review*, Nov–Dec 1992

Surprise

'... *the result of striking the enemy at a time or place, or in a manner, that he does not expect*.'

Key information or assessment:

- an understanding of what will surprise the enemy, for example timing, speed, place, technology
- an understanding of what force will be effective in achieving the objective.

Surprise, in the traditional military sense, has most closely been epitomised in corporate strategy during hostile takeovers. In the West, the jargon of hostile surprises has come into common corporate-finance parlance. 'Dawn raid', 'white knight', and 'poison pill' describe, respectively, surprise attack, salvation by a welcome ally, and legally structured share purchase and voting restrictions which thwart hostile acquisitions.

Security

'... the total of the measures a commander takes to prevent the surprise of his own forces and to keep the enemy in ignorance of his own plans and actions.'

Key information or assessment:

- the key elements of an organisation's plans that are relevant to the effective action of its people
- knowledge of the means by which its plans are leaked to rivals.

In the world of hostile takeovers, information analysts are one of the key influences on the outcome. High-security environments are created to prevent leaks of strategy and tactics in the court of the attacker and the defender. The players on both sides include accountants, merchant banks, media and public relations advisers and executives. The 'machines' on both sides crunch numbers and launch attacks and counter-attacks played out in the media and in the courts. They use the information to ask probing questions designed to influence shareholders, the Government and public opinion. 'How can the aggressor take over our client when it has such a poor management track-record itself?' they ask the shareholders and the general public.

Simplicity

'Orders must be concise and clear; plans must be perfectly comprehensive and direct.'

Key information or assessment:

- knowledge of the audiences
- the means of communication, and
- the context within which the orders will be received and delivered.

The king of Wu asked Sun Tzu to put his treatise on war to a simple test. The king's 180 concubines were brought out of the palace. Sun Tzu divided them into two groups with a favourite of the king's at the head of each group. He asked them if they knew the difference between front, back, left and right. They said yes. Sun Tzu instructed the concubines that when he issued a command they should obey. They assented. To the sound of drums playing, he ordered 'right turn'. The ladies only burst into laughter. He started again and gave a 'left turn' order. Again the ladies burst into laughter. Sun Tzu said, 'If the words of command are not clear and distinct, if orders are not thoroughly understood, the general is to blame. But, if his orders are clear and the soldiers nevertheless disobey, then it is the fault of their officers.' So saying, he ordered the leading ladies to be beheaded. Thereafter the concubines obeyed perfectly turning right and left, back and forth at each command.

Three other principles that Elting discusses are as follows.

Maintenance of morale

'... *troops with high morale are far more effective in combat.*'

Key information or assessment:

- information regarding the morale of the organisation's people
- knowledge of what would motivate its people to achieve the organisation's objectives.

Administration

'... *an army must be efficiently supplied and administered, the last including such matters as medical, pay, mail and personal records.*'

Key information or assessment:

- what back office support and services are required to support the front line operations and people.

Annihilation

'The Russians include annihilation among their Principles of War ... Annihilation has always been a feature of Oriental warfare. Genghis Khan, Tamerlane, and others of their ilk ... it was strategic bombing, especially with nuclear weapons, that really introduced annihilation to Western warfare as a definite strategy.'

Key information or assessment:

- what are the important aspects of the rivals' positions – their people, products, process, price, customers and/or regions
- how can an organisation attack the important positions or indeed all the positions of its rivals such that they lose heart and exit, ie sell their business to the organisation or close down their capacity.

The following sections describe the information required to make an effective response to the various situations that an organisation may face. The importance of strategic information and the role of tactics and tactical information is stressed throughout. A business would do well to remember the words of Carl von Clausewitz: 'Tactics is the art of using troops in battle; strategy is the art of using battles to win the war'.

ATTACK STRATEGIES

'It is the rule in war, if our forces are ten to the enemy's one, to surround him; if five to one, to attack him; if twice as numerous, to divide our army into two. If equally matched, we can offer battle; if slightly inferior in numbers, we can avoid the enemy; if quite unequal in every way, we can flee from him.'

Sun Tzu, *The Art of War*

This basic, 'rule of thumb' numeric assessment provides the simplest information requirements for deciding whether to attack or not. All that is needed is an assessment of the size and resources at the disposal of a competitor, its market share, cash reserves and access to capital.

The choices made regarding the breadth and depth or focus of a strategy are critical. Whom to have as friends and allies and whom to have as enemies; to attack or await attack, to retaliate or to withdraw – all determine the nature of competition and the profitability of an organisation's position.

Philip Kotler in *Marketing Management: Analysis, Planning, Implementation and Control* (Prentice Hall, 8th edn, 1994) points to a set of attack and defence strategies. Figure 17 below illustrates the attack options.

Figure 17   *Attack strategies*

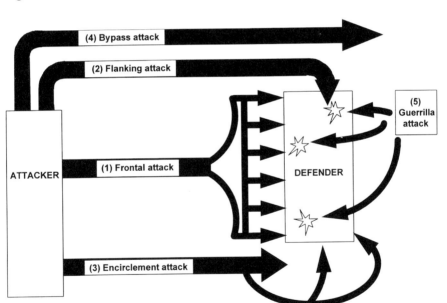

Kotler, Philip, MARKETING MANAGEMENT: Analysis, Planning, Implementation and Control, 8.e, © 1994, pp. 388, 395. Adapted by permission of Prentice Hall, Upper Saddle River, New Jersey.

Frontal attack

This involves attacking the rival's strengths rather than his weaknesses with the outcome depending on force and endurance. The key information required before committing to a frontal attack is:

- What are the factors that make the rival successful – people, product, prices, processes, advertising, etc
- What is the size of each of the rival's resources relative to your organisation's?

Kellogg cereals, over 70 years, has built itself a stronger reputation in Europe than in the US and other companies have followed suit. In some countries it commands 80% market share. However, General Mills stuck to the American market. Given that acquisitions of smaller players was costly, General Mills chose the joint-venture route to international expansion. It solicited the help of Nestlé to attack the $3.5 billion European cereals market and won approval to merge its European snack business with PepsiCo – making the combined group the market leader. This allowed it to benefit from established players' brand, distribution and marketing muscle, which could not be matched by a lone entrant.

Source: L. Therrien and C. Hoots, 'Café au lait, a croissant – and trix', *Business Week*, 24 August 1992

Flanking attack

This attack concentrates on the weaknesses of rivals. The key information required before committing to a flank attack is:

- What are the rival's weak people, products, customers, geographic areas, market segments
- What are the rival's weak processes, for example new products to market, distribution, customer service and support
- What are the rival's weak competences, for example marketing, engineering, technological development, sales?

Xerox invented office photocopiers. Canon attacked by introducing 90 new models, cutting Xerox's share in mid-range office copiers by half. The funds and position secured enable Canon to compete in the high-end colour copier market today. Canon effectively beat Xerox through creating a demand and recognising a weakness in Xerox's customer satisfaction. It gave the customer a range of choices so broad that the Xerox offering became a drop in the ocean in comparison. The main 'frontal' product, high-end colour copiers, was too difficult to attack directly and so its position in mid-range copiers was attacked instead.

Encirclement attack

This option involves launching an offensive on many fronts with the objective of breaking the rival's will to resist. The key information required before committing to an en- circlement attack is:

- What is the total market and all the segments and geographic areas in which the business competes with its rival
- What determines success in each of the segments and areas
- Do gaps in the satisfaction of customers exist in segments or areas
- What will it take to outcompete the rival on all fronts in terms of products, price, promotion, etc?

The information undertaking and how the other players encircled IBM through niche strategies

Throughout the early 1980s, IBM enjoyed a dominant position in its markets. Its massive mainframe strength allowed it to invest huge sums in research and development, sales, marketing and global distribution. Its position seemed insurmountable to itself and its rivals. In the lucrative and still-growing PC market the 'non-clone' manufacturers had dropped out and only Apple remained in an attempt to carve out a niche for itself.

In 1984, IBM took an undertaking to supply on-request information to agreed competitors enabling them to design systems compatible with IBM equipment. The undertaking was given to the European Commission after complaints that its dominant position in the information technology industry was harming competition. The voluntary undertaking included software and computer memory and avoided proceedings against IBM in what would have been one of the biggest anti-competition cases in the EC. In the intervening years IBM fell into a loss-making situation, Apple had the strongest hold on the PC market, smaller rivals such as Toshiba dominated the enormous laptop computer market, mainframe sales dropped away in favour of downsized mini- and workstations, and Hewlett Packard dominated the printer and peripherals markets. Niche strategies allowed rivals to take on the giant. In July of 1994, IBM announced: 'The information technology industry and numerous business practices have changed dramatically since we signed this undertaking in 1984 ... the dynamics of the industry have made most of the undertakings obsolete.'

Source: *Financial Times*, 8 July 1994

Bypass attack

Attacks on easier markets can create alternative sources of funds. Bypass attacks also involve creating fundamentally new ways of providing value and thereby change the rules of competition. The key information before committing to a bypass attack is:

- Can an organisation's products be sold to other markets?
- Can it sell other products to its current customers?
- Can it sell new products to new markets?
- Can it change its products, processes or ways of servicing customers to create a new market position?

Given the intensity of competition in the clothing industry in Europe, the removal of regional quotas and increase in the flexibility of quota utilisation in the European market was set to further intensify rivalry in the key UK and German markets. One of the key suppliers to both these countries was Hong Kong. What alternative strategy should be adopted to avoid harmful rivalry while achieving the objectives of growth and profit? The answer lies in the following bypass strategy:

- Targeting: the major Hong Kong houses already have high penetration of the UK and German market. Hence their targets should be France, Italy and Spain where their penetration is low.
- Making contact: the European market requires first-hand dealing. This is best achieved through the main European trade fairs.
- Market segments: fashion and tastes are diversified among Member States despite unification. The characteristics of each segment of the market need to be understood.
- Product: the premium commanded by branded products is high. The Hong Kong entrants will need to develop a brand strategy for their products and will need to increase the fashion content of the product.
- Supply chain: close links with buyers are essential. The key aspects determining the design of the supply-chain process are the need for flexibility to change fast in response to changes in customer preferences, shortened seasons, decreased delivery times and increased communication to provide higher service quality.
- IT: new technology becomes essential to provide manufacturing flexibility, a quick response and information for management.
- Longer term: in the longer term the Hong Kong houses may need to have a presence in sales, distribution and manufacturing. Given the need for fast response coupled with healthy margins the location for manufacturing could be one of the lower-cost countries, for example Portugal, Greece or Turkey.

Guerrilla attack
Small, intermittent attacks on different territories of the rival with the aim of harassing and demoralising him and thereby securing a permanent foothold. The tactics include selective price cuts, advertising intensely in one focused area, short-term cheap products, and legal actions.

The key information before committing to guerrilla attack is:

- What changes to the organisation's marketing mix will hurt the rival's position in the short term?
- What will divert the rival's management attention and frustrate him?

The US credit-card market is dominated by VISA International. In 1980, VISA and MasterCard were the only major competitors. By 1988, VISA had 115 million cards in circulation, MasterCard had 82 million, GE's Discover Card had 27 million and American Express had 24 million. By 1992, Discover Card had 39 million cards and MasterCard had 100 million cards. Discover Card had become nearly 40% of MasterCard's size compared to 33% in 1988. VISA continued to enjoy a leading position with 150 million cardholders.

In 1994, VISA's position was still very strong. Any new or established entrant could not attack VISA directly. The cost of creating the global card-issuing, merchant-acceptance and transaction-processing network was a real barrier to successful attack. Most market players add strength to VISA by 'co-branding' their cards, that is, labelling their cards with their own name as well as VISA's. The only way to attack VISA is to establish alternative products, pricing strategies and uses for the credit cards that are independent of VISA. Such guerrilla attacks are being launched from all sides and take the form of storecards, with retailer brands tapping into non-traditional channels for credit, such as supermarkets, fast food and healthcare. These guerrilla attacks allow a position to be developed by offering the customer incentives, such as discounts, bonus points for gifts and omitting the membership fee. Such incentives are difficult for VISA to offer as an organisation, although they can be offered by the VISA-licensed co-branding organisations. The use of guerrilla attacks is seen to be a good short-term tool to pressure a rival but in the longer-term one of the other attack strategies may be required to vanquish the rival.

Summary

Specific information of the type listed above is not as difficult to come by as might be imagined. The main sources of such information were described in Chapter One.

Your responsibility as leader is to ensure that you attack only if victory cannot be gained by other less damaging means, and that once you attack you follow through to victory. In conducting such attack strategies the business needs to be careful not to damage the profitability of the industry by creating a gap between customers' perceptions of what to expect and what can be delivered on a sustained basis.

Alternative strategies

Corporate strategists during the late 1980s adopted aggressive attack strategies including:

- hostile unsolicited takeovers
- price wars which drove down the profitability of much of UK industry
- alleged predatory pricing or dumping in Western countries which was bitterly contested by the US and Japanese governments
- dominant players, such as IBM, being fought by all comers on all fronts.

However, the end of the 1980s and early 1990s saw a surge of consolidation, collaborative and confrontation-avoidance strategies:

- Apple and IBM collaborated on the development of compatible operating systems
- the Big 8 international accounting firms became the Big 6 when KPMG formed from the merger of KMG Thomson McLintock and Peat Marwick Mitchell, and Coopers & Lybrand mostly merged with Deloitte Haskins & Sells.

In an article in the *Harvard Business Review* ('Collaborate with your competitors', November 1989) Hamel, Prahalad and Doz highlight four principles for **winning** through the collaborative expansion method:

(1)   Recognise that collaboration still requires a winning strategy. Action: have clear strategic objectives yourself and understand your rival's objectives.

(2) Do not avoid all conflict. Action: ensure that issues are resolved and success is measured and failure corrected.

(3) Place limits on co-operation. Action: some information, skills and technologies should be off-limits. This situation should be communicated, monitored and enforced.

(4) Learn from the partner. Action: to build skills implement a plan. Often these are skills outside the formal agreement.

'Hence to fight and conquer in all your battles is not supreme excellence; supreme excellence consists in breaking the enemy's resistance without fighting.'

Sun Tzu, *The Art of War*

DEFENCE STRATEGIES

'To secure ourselves against defeat lies in our own hands, but the opportunity of defeating the enemy is provided by the enemy himself.'

Sun Tzu, *The Art of War*

Kotler's illustration of defence strategies is given in Figure 18 below. The adoption of these strategies is dependent upon a number of key information requirements.

Figure 18 *Defence strategies*

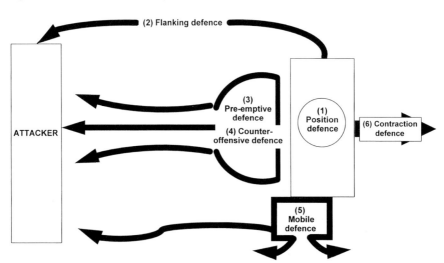

Kotler, Philip, MARKETING MANAGEMENT: Analysis, Planning, Implementation and Control, 8.e, © 1994, pp. 388, 395. Adapted by permission of Prentice Hall, Upper Saddle River, New Jersey.

Position defence

This defence involves building a strong position that cannot be penetrated by rivals. The key information to find out in order to erect defensive barriers to entry is:

- What are the investment requirements to push up the minimal efficient scale
- What are the factors that would differentiate the product
- How can the upfront capital investment requirement be increased for any new entrant setting up business in the industry
- What are the distribution channels that the organisation needs to tie to itself
- What are the cost drivers and how can cost advantages be gained that will be difficult to imitate, for example technology, location, government subsidies, learning curve
- What are the potential government actions required to limit entry, for example import restrictions, licensing requirements?

Flanking defence

The protection of a weakness, for example in product, customer satisfaction or process. The key information to find out in order to construct a good flanking defence is:

- What are the organisation's weaknesses?
- What are the threats it faces in each of these areas?
- What resources would be required to protect these weaknesses or resolve them?

A major food and drinks business gathered performance information to establish whether its speed of introduction of new 'product' or product variations was adequate relative to rivals. It discovered that it took twice the time of its rivals in responding to changes in customer demand. To protect itself from a potentially aggressive assault from rivals, the business invested in restructuring and technology improvements to halve its time to market.

Pre-emptive defence

Attacking the enemy before he attacks you. The key information to determine this 'offensive defence' is:

- What are the rival's motives and the market trends and gaps in satisfaction?
- What warnings would prevent the rival from attacking the organisation's market position?
- What are the initiatives available to take market share away from the rival and what impact would it have on the market, for example new products, use of new technologies, new promotional strategies?

The French and UK expectation is that the Channel Tunnel link between the two countries will result in the demise of the cross-Channel ferry companies. Given this impending doom how can a ferry company respond? P&O European Ferries has taken a pre-emptive combative approach using technology as the lever for providing high-quality service.

With daily traffic of 11,000 cars, 1,200 lorries and 63,000 people, the throughput across the Channel exceeds both Heathrow and Gatwick. To handle its share of this traffic P&O has invested £30 million in information technology. Some of the key investments are:

- A £5 million reservations system. This has installed 8,000 terminals in travel agents and operations throughout Europe that can dial P&O's system. The time to make a booking has been reduced to 3 seconds. The system offers hundreds of travel packages which can be targeted at specific customers and markets and, of course, automatically updates the sales ledger and issues a ticket.
- An auto-checking system. This will halve the current 45 minutes it takes to board 2,000 passengers by providing customers with a combined ticket and boarding pass, which can be verified by electronic readers. A typical airline takes 2 hours to board 400 passengers onto a plane.
- On-board point of sales systems allow fast processing of credit-card payments and transmit stock replenishment lists to enable stock to be ready at the quay side when the ferries come to port.

P&O invested to construct a pre-emptive defence and prevent an adverse outcome of cross-Channel competition. Its strategy was to create a competitive process to win and maintain customer loyalty. History shows that P&O and other Channel ferry operators have suffered huge losses in market share. However, the pre-emptive investments and joint ventures have slowed the loss of share.

Counter-offensive defence

Responding with a counter-attack after a rival has attacked. This may be to counter a product improvement, price cut, promotional push or distribution or geographical push. The key information to find out before launching a counter-offensive defence is:

- What has the rival just done to gain share or profits?
- What resources are available and affordable to match the rival?
- What are the rival's weaknesses?
- What are the alternative actions than can be taken to attack a weakness of the rival?

Mobile defence

This defence involves establishing a broad base to prevent rivals attacking in future. The options are to broaden the market coverage and/or market diversification. The key information to find out before deciding on a mobile defence is:

- What is the underlying need that the organisation's products and services satisfy and does it have the resources to satisfy this wider need?
- What are the related markets or regions that the organisation can satisfy with its current products or strengths?

Contraction defence

Withdrawing from products, markets and regions that are no longer attractive. The key information to find out before deciding to contract is:

- What are the organisation's weaknesses?
- Is there any strategic merit in remaining in these areas?
- Is it possible to retain a profitable and worthwhile position in the market, and if so, at what cost?

The high-stakes international soaps and detergent market has recently seen an attack and swift defence parry played between Unilever and Procter & Gamble. In 1994, Unilever announced the launch of a 'revolutionary' new detergent throughout Europe. The UK name was Persil Power and the Dutch name Omo Power. Unilever confidently announced that the results of this 10-year research investment represented a major technological breakthrough and that $150 million had been invested in product facilities.

	Unilever	*Procter & Gamble*
pre-1989	20% market share	24% market share
1989	Small advantage in Europe	Large advantage in US
1994	23% market share	32% market share

The table above shows how Unilever has failed to keep pace with Procter & Gamble's growth in the $25 billion world fabric detergent market. Persil Power was its attempt to catch up.

Some research into the rival product's performance at high temperatures, for which it was not designed or intended, gave Procter & Gamble the answer as to how to block Unilever's move. Procter & Gamble in Holland widely publicised a claim that Persil Power rotted clothes because it was too powerful. Unilever threatened a law suit. Several independent tests later Unilever dropped the suit and said it would 'reformulate' the product.

Millions of pounds, years of investment and consumer goodwill are easily destroyed if every aspect of the attack is not watertight from a wiley competitor. Procter & Gamble managed to make a strong counteroffensive defence that achieved two things – it left the attacker's resources focused on nursing its wounds whilst allowing the defender to gain ground. It is certain that this is not the end of the moves between these two players – news of a retaliatory move in the near future should be expected.

Source: 'Talk from the washroom' *The Economist*, 11 June 1994

RETALIATION STRATEGIES

'*Injuring all of a man's 10 fingers is not as effective as chopping off one, and routing 10 enemy divisions is not as effective as annihilating one of them.*'

Mao Tse-tung

Mao's tactics demoralised the enemy and provided a harvest of captured weapons. Mao fought only when the odds were in his favour and there was a certainty of winning. His attacks and his retaliation were intended to damage his enemies, provide him with additional strength as well as send a clear message of his determination not to quit.

Retaliation is the key to determining whether an attack strategy leads to success or failure. Retaliation is also the key to whether an organisation's rivals will succeed in their attacks upon its position. The basic information required for retaliation is common to all the strategic issues described in this book – knowledge of the organisation's rivals, the organisation itself and those that can influence it.

The key information to seek out in determining whether rivals will retaliate is:

- what resources they have available
- the seriousness of the threat of the organisation's attack on their position and the level of commitment they have to a long-term position in the market
- whether retaliation will expose an area for the organisation to attack
- the rational or emotional nature of the rival
- the intensity of rivalry
- the clarity and focus of the rival's strategy
- the regulatory constraints.

The key information to seek out to prepare for retaliation is:

- what the objective of the retaliation will be
- what 'liquid' resources can be committed to a counter-attack
- the speed with which the organisation will retaliate
- the toughness of its retaliation
- the commitment of its people to retaliate
- the weakness of the rival that will be attacked.

IN THIS CHAPTER

We drew on lessons from military strategy on the principles of attack, defence and retaliation. Sun Tzu and Philip Kotler helped to examine the attack and defence strategies available and the information needed to act. Swift and serious retaliation applied with determination was seen to be critical to influencing a rival's future actions. The principles of the chapter are summarised in Figure 19 below.

Figure 19   *Responding: attack, defence and retaliatory strategies*

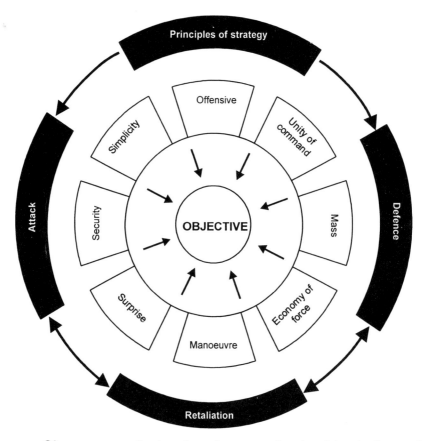

Given any particular situation, your leadership challenge is to head bold attacks, create unassailable defences and deliver crippling retaliations. Without such determination competitors will not allow you to be the master of your own destiny.

The next chapter will examine the information needed to execute tactics successfully. We will examine the importance of picking the battle and the enemy, acting opportunistically and moving fast to the attack. The role of messages, signals and disinformation will also be explored.

LEADERSHIP CHALLENGE
FIVE

*Manoeuvre your rivals
not just your own organisation*

Chapter Five

MANOEUVRING: ADOPT TACTICS

'*Do not repeat the tactics which have gained you one victory, but let your methods be regulated by the infinite variety of circumstances.*'

Sun Tzu, *The Art of War*

INTRODUCTION

If an organisation responds to market changes and competitor moves, then predictably it is laying itself open to defeat from a rival who monitors the response and who himself has unconventional and therefore unpredictable tactics. This chapter will establish the techniques for fast-response tactical manoeuvre, building on this by establishing how to create opportunities and the information needed to do so. We will then examine how to spot and seize opportunities. Time-based strategy, speed of response and surprise have all been recognised by the business gurus as critical to gaining and building competitive advantage. The age-old military principles behind these tactics will be briefly discussed to distil the key information requirements. Finally, we will explore the role of communication and the use of signalling to inform and misinform the competition.

We will begin by taking a look at the role that you, the leader, must play to meet the challenge. The lesson on the critical success factors in the use of tactics is from Michael Dell.

MEETING CHALLENGE FIVE

To meet the leadership challenge you must demonstrate the ability to manoeuvre out of unfavourable situations and into winning ones. The key leadership quality to meet this challenge is possessing sharp and swift **neural processes**. The key mental attributes you need in order to meet the challenge are:

- clarity of thought
- speed of processing information, and
- an ability to learn quickly and constantly.

This needs to be backed up by highly developed **relationship management** qualities, particularly the attributes of game playing, toughness in action and thought, ability to shape people's expectations, and energy and endurance. In turn, this needs to be reinforced with the quality of visualising potential outcomes.

Leadership entails significant responsibilities. These include ensuring that:

- information is gathered on the rivals and the terrain
- assessments must be made as to whether it is better to fight or tactically withdraw, and
- capabilities must be created, such as speed, surprise and innovation.

If you cannot discharge this responsibility you will fight battles that are not worth fighting and lose ones that should be won. This is irresponsible and will waste your organisation's talents and resources.

MICHAEL DELL (1965–   )

Michael Dell is the young founder and CEO of the Dell Computer Corporation. His business is based on securing a direct sales relationship with the customer by cutting out the intermediary channels. He started his company at the age of 19, setting up all aspects of this business himself, including freight negotiation, warehousing rental and advertising design. In 1994 his sales approached $3.5 billion with profits of $149 million and 6,500 employees.

Dell's strategy was simple: to sell personal computers directly to the customer, removing the middle-men. The tactics by which he won allowed him to take market share, profits and positions away from giants such as IBM and Compaq. His tactics include building products to order, enabling him to minimise stock levels; his factories give him the flexibility to supply customised products in order sizes of one; toll-free numbers allow customers to access his own telesales staff; delivery is made within days by outsourced distributors; combining products of industry specialists enables him to minimise research and development expenditure whilst maximising focus on where he chooses to add value; leased premises allow him to minimise fixed costs allowing sales to asset ratios of 10 to 15 times bigger rivals. Dell has created an unmatched capability that allows him to focus on the market-place tactics of price, responsiveness and value-adding add-on sales. This capability cannot be rivalled by larger and clumsier competitors with high overheads. At 30, his personal stake in Dell Computers was valued at around $473 million. Whilst competitors look at the industry from an engineering technology of futuristic perspective, Dell focuses with passion on satisfying the customer's needs. He believes success comes from speed in reaching the customer with new products. If product development times are slow the opportunity to make an impact is lost. He is quoted as saying 'If you stop, you're dead basically. In this business, there are two kinds of people, really, the quick and the dead' (Farkas, De Backer and Sheppard *Maximum Leadership* (Orion Books)).

STRENGTHS AND WEAKNESSES

'*You can be sure of succeeding in your attacks if you only attack places which are undefended. You can ensure the safety of your defence if you only hold positions that cannot be attacked.*'

Sun Tzu, *The Art of War*

Both Sun Tzu and Miyamoto Musashi pointed to the importance of picking the field of battle and the opponent, and then joining the attack with eyes open to the tactical manoeuvres that will secure victory. This section will examine the importance of understanding strengths and weaknesses in deciding what to attack, and the importance of technique in winning battles.

Your responsibility as a leader extends to ensuring that your organisation goes beyond the battle at hand and creates and seizes opportunities along the way.

What to attack

An analysis of strengths and weaknesses is critical to allocating resources: an organisation should not move unless it has a good understanding of the opportunities and threats facing it.

Chapter Three examined the types of information required to assess strengths and weaknesses. Such information is useful in creating an agenda for improving weak areas. The standard recommendations in most management texts advise working on weaknesses and matching strengths against the opportunities in the external environment; more practical situational guidance is not usually forthcoming. To prepare an attack or defence against rivals, there is a need to understand their strengths and weaknesses in terms of resources, products, coverage, competences, capabilities and alliances: what they are good at and not so good at.

Most management texts are unclear as to how this information is to be applied in a competitive situation. However, Sun Tzu explains in *The Art of War* what additional information is required and what should be done once it is obtained. Table 6 below presents the information and actions that can be taken in a business context.

Table 6   *Information about a rival and appropriate action*

Information	Action
Stability: Is your rival content with his position?	Attack his market position
Resource strength: Is your rival well resourced?	Acquire his resources, eg hire his key people
Weaknesses: What are your rival's weak areas?	Attack them
Attack plans: Is your rival preparing to attack your position, eg through a big promotion or price-cutting war?	Distract his attention, eg with a legal battle
Movements: What are your rival's plans and likelihood of success?	Hide your plans and focus your attack on one or a few key areas that will divide his efforts, eg introduce a rival product first

An analysis of the strengths and weaknesses of an organisation and its rivals is essential to enable the principle of mass and economy of force to be applied.

Technique

Without straying too far into an exploration of strategy and tactics at the expense of information, we will briefly look at the guidelines of Miyamoto Musashi regarding the application of technique.

According to Musashi the critical objective is to forestall the enemy. The three methods of achieving this are by attacking, *Ken No Sen*; forestalling the enemy's attack, *Tai No Sen*, ie upon being attacked to counter-attack; and attacking the enemy at the same time as his attack on you, *Tai Tai No Sen*.

In Figure 20 below the techniques to be used in battle are illustrated. The implications, as described by Musashi, of the application of the techniques are as follows.

Figure 20   *Techniques for real-time action and reaction*

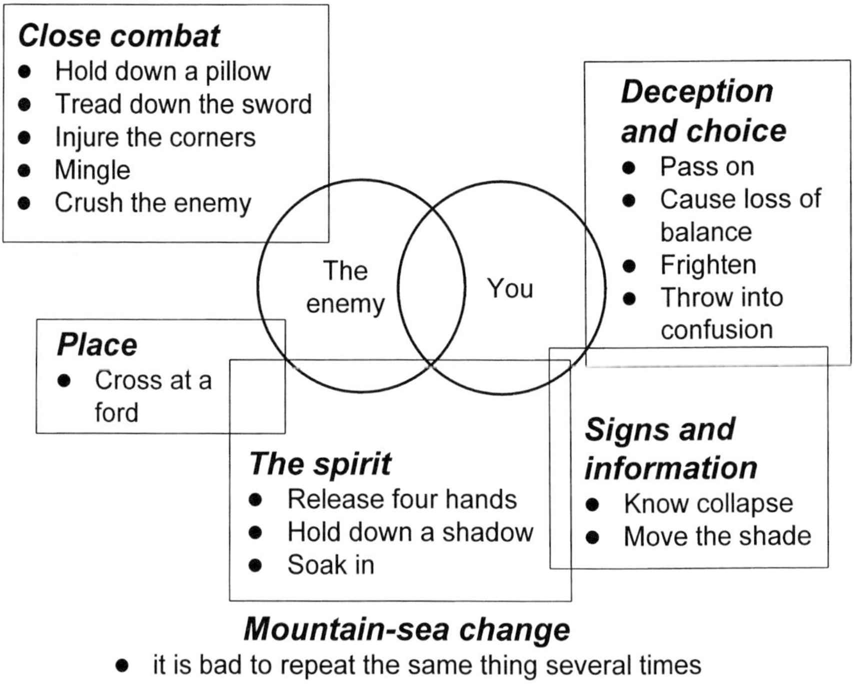

Close combat
- Hold down a pillow
- Tread down the sword
- Injure the corners
- Mingle
- Crush the enemy

Deception and choice
- Pass on
- Cause loss of balance
- Frighten
- Throw into confusion

The enemy

You

Place
- Cross at a ford

The spirit
- Release four hands
- Hold down a shadow
- Soak in

Signs and information
- Know collapse
- Move the shade

Mountain-sea change
- it is bad to repeat the same thing several times

Close combat
- '**To hold down a pillow** means not allowing the enemy's head to rise.'
- '**To tread down the sword** . . . you should not aspire just to strike him, but to cling on after the attack.'
- '**To injure the corners** . . . It is difficult to move strong things by pushing directly, so you should "injure the corners".'
- '**To mingle** . . . in confrontation, attack the enemy's strong points and, when you see that they are beaten back, quickly separate and attack yet another strong point on the periphery of his force.'
- '**To crush the enemy** regarding him as being weak.'

Place
- '**Crossing at a ford** . . . at the advantageous place, as a good sea captain crosses a sea route.'

Deception and choice

- '**To pass on** ... when the enemy is agitated and shows an inclination to rush ... make a show of complete calmness ... when you can see that his spirit has passed on ... [attack] strongly.'
- '**To cause loss of balance** ... attack without warning where the enemy is not expecting it ...'
- '**To frighten** ... caused by the unexpected' – words, size of force, flank attack.'
- '**To throw into confusion**. This means making the enemy lose resolve.'

Signs and information

- '**To know collapse** ... when the enemy starts to collapse you must pursue him without letting the chance go.'
- '**To move the shade** is used when you cannot see the enemy's spirit ... indicate that you are about to attack strongly, to discover his resources.'

The spirit

- '**To release four hands** ... [when] the issue cannot be decided ... win with a spirit the enemy does not expect.'
- '**To hold down a shadow** is used when you can see the enemy's attacking spirit ... if you make a show of strongly suppressing his technique, he will change his mind.'
- '**To soak in** ... become one with the enemy ... mutually entangled.'

Mountain-sea change

- '... it is bad to repeat the same thing several times.'

In addition to the up-to-the-minute information requirements implied by the above moves and countermoves, Musashi advises thinking deeply on the basis of certain additional knowledge to fight in the *spirit* of strategy. The additional information required is:

- the enemy's disposition in battle – whether it is flourishing or waning

- knowing enough about the enemy in his situation to be able to 'think yourself into the enemy's position'
- the 'depths' of the enemy, to be able to 'destroy the enemy's spirit in its depth'.

When entangled, Musashi advises stepping back and looking for alternative means of achieving the goals. He also suggests thinking of the enemy as your own troops; yours to manoeuvre at will.

Musashi's exposition of the techniques for fast-moving combat is comprehensive and these techniques are especially appropriate for very dynamic, emerging or highly competitive markets. Musashi is an interesting mix of both killer and philosopher, explaining close combat and large-scale strategy and then considering the deeper meaning of 'the Way' of strategic thinking. A more conventional analysis will be applied below, where the key messages of timing, surprise and speed are clarified.

ART OF OPPORTUNISM

'Anyone can plan a campaign, but few are capable of waging war, because only a true military genius can handle the developments and circumstances.'

Napoleon

Long-term strategic intent or the determination of business direction has been explored in Chapter Three, and Chapter Four examined the information needed to fuel the strategies and tactics of attack, defence and retaliation. Long-term strategic intent aside, competitive strategy involves the pursuit of seizing and creating opportunities to win. Whilst strategies need to be adapted to changing circumstances, tactics need to be planned but constantly adapted to the opportunities arising from rivals' moves and countermoves.

The practice of the art of opportunism is one that determines actual success or failure. Strategies and plans are all very well but without being *close to the situation* and therefore playing tactics that reflect the unfolding situation you are merely an armchair general. Advantages are gained over rivals in the front-line by the moves and countermoves made against them.

This section examines the art of opportunism. The art involves the creation of opportunities and the exploitation of those that others create. In order to create opportunities you must have a good understanding of the rival, intelligence on his position and an idea of how to manoeuvre him into a position that allows him to be defeated. An important initial objective is to draw the rival out and allow him to expose his weaknesses. In order to benefit from an opportunity created by others, there must be the intelligence to identify the opportunity, the knowledge of what is required to seize opportunities and the nimbleness of foot or readiness of resources to seize the opportunity. A real-time action and reaction capability is critical, and the techniques described by Miyamoto Musashi above are of great relevance.

Creating opportunities

'All warfare is based on deception.'

Sun Tzu, *The Art of War*

The 'heaven-born captain' endeavours not to be at the mercy of chance: he creates his own luck. Table 7 below provides an analysis of the information needed to be received and given to create opportunities. The creation of completely new opportunities is a critical endeavour if your organisation is to lead and shape its own future. Your responsibility as leader is to ensure that your organisation also gives priority to creative endeavours.

In this context, 'attack' means undertaking any indirect activity which would threaten the position or focus of rivals. The following direct marketing devices serve an organisation in repositioning itself, allowing it to seize market share: changing products and attributes; their price; how they are promoted; through which intermediaries and channels of distribution; their geographic coverage; and to which target customers.

Table 7 *Information needed to create opportunities*

Information to collect	Information to give	Action/opportunity	Corporate example
Are you ready to attack?	Seem unable to attack	Attack	Launch a new product
Are you deploying your resources to gain position?	Seem inactive	Continue attack	Develop a new product secretly
What will entice your rival to attack?	Hold out the bait	Attack	Enter your rival's major market with a lower-priced equivalent
Is your rival prone to aggression?	Entice him to attack	Let him dissipate resources	Make a bid for another rival to entice a counter-offer
Does your rival believe you are strong?	Pretend to be weak	Attack with force	Announce a lack of resources to copy rivals
Are your rival's resources well organised?		Disrupt them	Hire your rival's key staff
Is your rival pleased with his position and therefore inactive?		Harass him	Issue legal suits

Sainsbury's, one of the biggest UK high-street retailers, introduced a new 'fighting brand' of cola to compete with Coke in the summer of 1993. Up to that point Coca-Cola's Coke and other brands had about 80% of the market share and Sainsbury's previous own brand had about 20%. Within the launch week Sainsbury's managed to turn the table in market-share terms with Coke. The Sainsbury's product had similar packaging to Coca-Cola's original, diet and caffeine-free Cokes and, according to some 'off the cuff' tests, similar taste. A change was negotiated to the design a short while later but was clearly conceived by Sainsbury's to do little to change the similarities. Pepsi had invested millions fighting Coke over the years. Sainsbury's achieved far more with far less investment. Sainsbury's had made two important achievements:

- It had held out the bait. If this bait had been taken by the brand manufacturers in a fight over market share through price, litigation or some other means, an even more damaging industry precedent might have been set with the ensuing publicity.
- It had given a clear message to manufacturers of branded products: do not seek to enter a battle you cannot win; play on our terms.

As can be seen from Table 7, the use of information collected to give messages and signals to rivals to encourage them to 'take the bait' creates opportunities to take the advantage.

Seizing opportunities

Sun Tzu's 'heaven-born captain' is also an opportunist who is prepared to 'seize the moment'. Table 8 below provides an analysis of the information an organisation needs to collect in order to keep its eyes and ears open and seize opportunities.

Table 8 *Information needed to seize opportunities*

Information to collect	Action/opportunity	Corporate examples
Important intentions of rivals	Arrive before the rival	New product development
Small players who lack the resources to sustain position/ Rivals of your rivals with resources	Make alliances	Joint ventures, alliances, EDI links
Gaps in territories	Enter a new territory	New markets or regions
Dissatisfied people in your rival's organisation	Entice them to work for you	Recruit key employees
Weak position of rivals	Launch an attack on your rival's position	Funding problems faced by your rival
Dissatisfied subjects	Encourage them to switch sides	Win over dissatisfied customers
Opportunities in neighbouring territories	Seize new territories to fund exploits in existing	Short-term, high-yield investments

Table 8 above illustrates a range of opportunities that can be seized depending on the changes in circumstances in the market. The same marketing devices described above are also available to an organisation to reposition itself and seize market share. Your responsibility as leader is to ensure that such opportunities are sought out and exploited.

As can be seen from Table 8, the method of seizing opportunities is by using information collected to move quickly and surreptitiously to the organisation's benefit and its rival's detriment. The case of Nirma versus Hindustan Lever in the massive Indian detergent market illustrates how a smaller player seized opportunities to consolidate its position and win against a much larger giant.

In 1969, Mr Karsandbhai Patel decided to augment his government salary by selling inexpensive laundry detergent powder. He mixed the powder in a 12-square-yard room in his home town of Ahmadabad and cycled around the neighbourhood selling his product on a bicycle. Hindustan Lever, the Indian joint-venture business of Unilever, was the market leader in detergents with its top brand, Surf.

In 1989 the *Financial Review*, 17 July 1989, reported that in 20 years Mr Patel's company, Nirma, had won 58% of India's 950,000 tonne, $520 million market. A clear turning point to enable Mr Patel to gain share and position was the opportunity presented to him by Hindustan Lever. Top Hindustan Lever executives felt sufficiently alarmed in the early 1980s to order a 'survey' of housewives in a downtown area of Bombay*. Under the guise of market researchers Lever employees were distributing packets of Nirma powder and leaflets and asking for completed questionnaires relating to the product. One such sales person chanced upon the house of Nirma's employees. In the local police station the sales woman admitted she was doing research for Hindustan Lever. A formal complaint for trade violation was filed. Just over a month later Hindustan Lever settled out-of-court and Mr Patel promptly seized the opportunity to pour the money into a massive national television and cinema advertising campaign.

*Source: 'A soapy scrap', *World Executive Digest*, May 1989

REAL-TIME INFORMATION AND REACTION

'You win in battles with the timing in the Void born of the timing of cunning by knowing the enemies' timing, and thus using a timing which the enemy does not expect.'
Miyamoto Musashi, Go Rin No Sho (1645)

If historic competitive strategy can be likened to a game of chess with considered sequential moves and counter-moves, modern competitive strategy can be likened to a computer game with emphasis on speed of attack and counter-attack, and the ability to move and fire rapidly and simultaneously with both hands.

Technique, timing and speed are critical success factors in such fast-moving fights. The importance of time for strategy, tactics and operational improvement is clearly understood by many companies. Various techniques are employed to achieve time compression such as just-in-time, business process re-engineering and various process-simplification techniques based on critical path analysis. The importance of speed and surprise are also closely linked to timing and are well understood.

Time-based strategy

As far as timing is concerned, there are those that move first and those that follow.

First movers have a free hand to:

- tie up best suppliers and channels
- occupy the best locations
- establish their brands
- secure patents
- build customer loyalty and tie them into their products and services.

To exploit these advantages the first mover needs to plan his strategy carefully and completely to ensure that he can seize as many of the advantages as possible before entrants reduce the profitability of the market. Information needs to be gathered on the potential suppliers and channels, best locations, customers and the ways in which they can be tied to their products.

Late-mover advantages include:

- the ability to copy and develop the products of existing players
- the opportunity to learn from the mistakes of early movers
- buying the latest plant and equipment
- buying a well-trained workforce from rivals.

All these factors determine the cost of entry and establishing position. Time is a critical factor in reducing these costs.

Mars plc entered the UK ice-cream market with its established confectionery brands. First-mover advantages seized included establishing its freezer units in all the small outlets first; creating a demand for high-quality, real-cream ice cream in a market where the majority of consumers were used to eating lower-quality ice creams; and adoption of established confectionery market strategies (20% extra free, buy packets of six and get one free, small 'fun-size' bars). The critical advantage was timing and speed. The critical information was:

- knowledge of the slowness of the rivals in deciding to enter the market; estimated time once decisions were taken to create appropriate products; creating marketing strategies; and applying the logistics to reach the market shelves
- information regarding consumer tastes and demand to identify the various market segments
- analysis of existing market players, products and coverage – this enabled Mars to differentiate its product.

Timing allowed Mars to capture and exploit the market with no competitors and then attack each new entrant from a position of strength. Sun Tzu's **narrow pass** strategy had been created and Mars had succeeded in occupying all the best spots above the pass.

Speed and surprise
Military history provides some spectacular instances of surprise and speed as decisive factors in victory.

Alexander the Great's conquests provide many examples of speed and surprise.

At the age of 20 when Alexander seized the throne, following the assassination of his father, he began a campaign to secure the lands within and around Macedonia. Hearing of his credibility being undermined in Thebes, Alexander undertook a tremendous forced march down Macedonia's western border to Thebes and within a week of arriving had begun the 'swiftest and greatest disaster' which had ever befallen a Greek city.

Later, in his first attack on the Persian army, Alexander crossed the River Granicus at night, stole a march by night and clashed with and slaughtered the Persians whose practice was not to begin a march before sunrise.

Alexander marched to confront Darius, the Persian king, at Issus. By chance, Darius took a circuitous route and appeared behind Alexander only one day's march away. Darius had six times as many soldiers. Alexander in a bold and swift move turned his army around, confronted the Persian army on the bank of the River Issus and, through a combination of defence and direct attack designed to reach Darius himself, broke the will of the Persians and defeated them.

Alexander then marched to Egypt and conquered the coastal plains. Gaza, the ancient Philistine city, presented a formidable defence perched high atop a hill. Alexander's solution was characteristic. Since the city was too high, then the ground level had to be raised to meet it. A mound 400 feet wide and 250 feet high was built (probably a Macedonian exaggeration), which enabled the walls to be scaled and Gaza taken. Alexander had forced through an innovative solution to take a formidable position.

For timing to be fully exploited it must be accompanied by speed and surprise. The examples described above illustrate this principle extremely well as practised by one of history's great strategists. From Alexander the Great, we can draw some important lessons:

- **surprise** your rivals by appearing in force where you are not expected
- **break the unwritten rules** that inhibit rivals
- **innovate** to attack what is perceived to be impregnable.

The information required is on the location of the rival, his code of operation, the strength of his position and the resources at his disposal.

MESSAGES – SIGNS AND SIGNALS

'As a captured North Vietnamese officer explained in 1966, "Americans are naive ... and do not know what is happening to them ... newspapers, radios, magazines, and television are all instruments of war".'
                                    J.R. Elting, *The Superstrategists*

Messages are sent to the external world in many ways, principally through:

- the media – newspapers, radios, magazines, billboards, direct mail and television – all fast becoming global communication channels especially as the more 'repressive' governments of the world are overthrown by their people, who subsequently open their arms to the world's products, services and media
- action or inaction, which signals the degree of commitment; this will be explored in more detail below
- 'doomed spies', as described above (p 64), who can be used to pass disinformation to rivals.

These signals can be bluffs, warnings or true commitments. How can you know which of these you are receiving? The answer lies in knowing rivals well enough to judge the credibility of the messages and signals they are sending. Competitor analysis, described in Chapter Three, provides a framework for assessing the likely meaning of messages and implications. However, to guard against the application of such logical frameworks by *your* rivals to predict *your* messages and signals you need to be secretive and practise deception regularly. It all sounds rather complex!

So what do these messages mean? And can an organisation rely on the information it is being sent? As the objectives of this type of information are so diverse, it is worthwhile making an investment to understand rivals, tracking their signals and the actual actions they take. Care must be taken about the number of other factors that can add 'noise', such as changes in board directors, advertising agencies or management consultants.

The range of information from such messages includes:

- warnings or threats of retaliation
- tests of rival's commitment to match moves
- encouraging mirroring of moves
- advance warnings to avoid damaging industry profit-ability
- communicating to the stakeholders and public at large
- building internal support
- falsehoods where there is no intention of doing any-thing at all
- verification of actions and explanation of rationale
- celebration of success
- show of strength
- show of commitment
- revealing assumptions and beliefs about the future of the industry
- influencing the future nature of the industry.

The basic questions to ask yourself are:

- Do you believe the message and its implications?
- Is your position threatened?
- Do you need to pre-empt or retaliate?
- Do you need to demonstrate commitment in some other way?
- Do you need to copy the move to maintain your position?

Michael Porter in *Competitive Strategy* highlights a number of market signals that can be classified as talk and action.

Talk
- prior announcement of moves
- announcement of results or actions after the fact
- public discussions of the industry by competitors
- competitors' discussions and explanations of their own moves.

Action

- competitors' tactics relative to what they could have done
- manner in which strategic changes are initially implemented
- divergence from past goals
- divergence from industry precedent
- the cross-parry
- the fighting brand
- private anti-trust suits.

The range of information conveyed by such action-oriented messages includes:

- conciliation by taking a less aggressive stance, for example on advertising
- signalling an intent to force a war, for example a price war
- refocus of the business, indicating a change in assumptions
- a warning of intent to protect position at any cost
- harassment
- tests of rival's commitment to match moves
- show of strength
- show of commitment
- changing the future nature of the industry.

Action, as opposed to just talk, has some certainty to it. It is at least a commitment of resources. However, do not be fooled into taking actions at face value. Rivals may be willing to make false moves; demonstrate a commitment that they do not have; draw you out to defend a position and so enable them to attack another position. Therefore, without an understanding of the rival and an investment made in tracking his signals and the actual actions taken, it is difficult to interpret his moves. Reference to Table 7 on p 126 will give you an indication of some of the deceptive actions rivals may take.

*IN THIS CHAPTER*_____

Lessons were learnt from Miyamoto Musashi, Sun Tzu, Alexander the Great and many corporations. An understanding of strengths and weaknesses makes for successful attack and defence, and the faster the change, the more critical the need to gather real-time information to enable fast reaction.

The need for fast response to the world around us was recognised – competition is not a static game. Diverse tactics may be required to win. The art of opportunism is seen to be an imperative and often relies on the collection of information of direct and indirect relevance to business. This information needs to be interpreted with some insight into the rival's psychology and the nature of the environment in which businesses compete.

The role of messages and signals was seen to be an important tool of communicating intent and of propaganda and deception. It was also found that the distinction between action and talk provides no certainty as to the intent of rivals. Insight, experience and skills are needed to distinguish between the different types of messages in action and talk. Based on these assessments there is a need to attack, defend or retaliate. Other opportunistic tactics of collusion, alliance and diversification should be seized to multiply resources at opportune times. As Sun Tzu points out, success will depend on the knowledge of five key points:

'(1) *He will win who knows when to fight and when not to fight.*
 (2) *He will win who knows how to handle both superior and inferior forces.*
 (3) *He will win whose army is animated by the same spirit throughout its ranks.*
 (4) *He will win who, prepared himself, waits to take the enemy unprepared.*
 (5) *He will win who has the military capacity and is not interfered with by the sovereign.*'

The principles of the chapter are illustrated in Figure 21 below.

Figure 21 *Manoeuvring: adopt tactics*

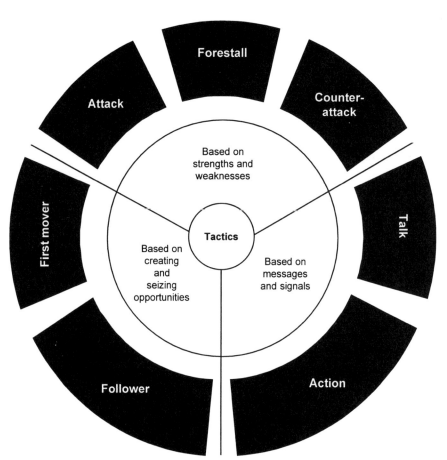

Your leadership challenge is to ensure that your organisation is able to manoeuvre into situations where it can win and to be swift in creating and seizing such opportunities. If you fail to seize the initiative you will forgo profits to your rivals' benefit.

The next chapter enters the boardroom. The macro-level information, the knowledge of the organisation, its rivals and position are drawn together with the information required to compete in a dynamic world to paint a picture for the executive and enable him to transform, redesign, manage change, benchmark to peers and assess the value of his organisation's activities.

LEADERSHIP CHALLENGE
SIX

Draw up an agenda to lead your organisation to victory now and to get to the future first

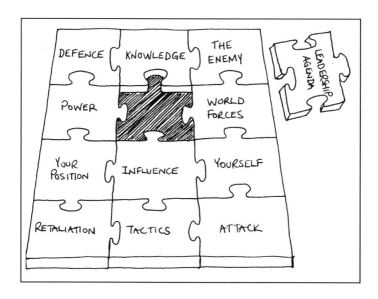

Chapter Six

EXECUTIVE DECISION-MAKING: CREATE AND MANAGE CHANGE

'*Measurement owes its existence to Earth; estimation of quantity to measurement; calculation to estimation of quantity; balancing of chances to calculation; and victory to balancing of chances.*'

Sun Tzu, *The Art of War*

INTRODUCTION

If the root cause of victory is measurement then it is essential to measure. Measuring will enable a business to estimate the size of the factors affecting success, which will enable it to calculate the chance of success. In turn, this will allow a business to balance the chance of success and failure and decide its course of action.

This chapter will draw together the key themes explored in this book to demonstrate how they fit into the context of an executive agenda for shaping the future of your organisation and for creating and managing change in an organisation. The following agenda items must be discharged:

- Agenda item one: gaining knowledge and information – regarding the environment, the organisation, its enemies and relative position. This allows a business to establish the case for change.
- Agenda item two: developing purpose, strategies and tactics – regarding an organisation's vision of the future and the strategies and tactical manoeuvres required to achieve its vision. This allows a business to develop its vision and goals.
- Agenda item three: developing a programme of change – regarding products and services, processes and systems, people and resources, relationships and structure, and values and culture. This allows a business to articulate with clarity the programme of change it believes is required to achieve its vision.

- Agenda item four: developing the information to monitor and fuel change – regarding the world around us from a management and executive point of view. This provides a business with the information it needs to manage change.
- Agenda item five: developing self. This allows a business to renew itself and create the leadership qualities that will enable it to produce and manage change.

The focus of this chapter will be on the information required to create and manage change rather than the change process itself.

Just as in previous chapters, we will begin by taking a look at the role that you, the leader, must play to meet the challenge. This challenge is one that requires you to have been able to meet all previous challenges. The lesson in outstanding corporate leadership comes from GE's Jack Welch.

MEETING CHALLENGE SIX

To meet the leadership challenge you must demonstrate the ability to create an agenda to win now and lead your organisation to the future first. To do this all the key leadership qualities are required:

- **values and beliefs** that are deeply held, passionate and committed and based upon sound reasoning
- **neural processes** that give you the advantage of clarity, speed and breadth
- the ability to **visualise** potential futures, and
- **relationship management** skills to enable you to plan and enact strategies to steer industries, organisations and people.

Leadership entails significant responsibilities. As the leader you must ensure that:

- the articulated case for change is compelling
- the information net is wide and alive to changes in the world around you
- opportunities are created, identified and harnessed
- a holistic view of change is taken
- the organisation is challenged through benchmarks and experiences
- the organisation is mobilised and then sustained for the challenge
- your own self is regularly renewed.

If you cannot discharge these responsibilities, you should reassess your suitability to be the leader.

JACK WELCH (1935–)

Jack Welch was born in Massachusetts, USA, in a poor neighbourhood. A tough boy, he learned to fight, compromise and charm. In the streets where he played and organised inter-city games, he was known as a fearless negotiator and an aggressive competitor. He went on to graduate in chemical engineering, taking an MSc and a PhD.

In 1960, he joined General Electric's chemical business. Welch's style was competitive and atypical. In 1972, he was made a vice-president and in 1973 a vice-president in the group's components and materials business. Welch was considered a maverick and in 1975 when the company compiled its list of its top 30 managers he was not on the list. However, he continued to move up the corporate ladder and in 1981 became the chairman and chief executive of the company. Welch inherited a company that was trying to be all things electrical, from toasters to jet engines. Its businesses were bureaucratically run, largely insulated from global competition and were able to survive despite their variable margins.

Welch proceeded to introduce a series of changes that would ultimately transform the business. His vision was to build a company with the reach and resources of a big company and the entrepreneurial nature of a small company. He wanted this company to be a leader in its chosen markets. The first change was to have a lasting and profound impact on the ambitions and performance of the company. He gathered his executives together and instructed them that GE would only be involved in businesses that were, or could be, number one or two in their global markets. 'The rest were to be fixed, sold or closed.' In the 1980s, GE invested $10 billion and through acquisition $19 billion to strengthen the businesses of the future. This restructuring was reinforced through delaying to clear out the bureaucracy. These two moves allowed him to 'change the hardware'.

Welch and his team then proceeded to 'change the software'. This involved introducing three cultural attributes – self-confidence, simplicity and speed. This programme was reinforced by a number of changes. First, behaviour was changed by involving everyone in group-learning and problem-solving sessions called 'work-outs'. Secondly, managers were categorised into four types, plotted in a four-by-four matrix with 'Fit to GE's Values' on one axis and 'Performance' on the other. Those that did not perform or fit the values were dismissed. Those that performed but did not fit the values were also dismissed. GE's Management Institute was used to share experiences, aspirations and frustrations across thousands of managers. Its 130 high-ranking executives became involved in a management development programme said to rival the US military. These changes allowed GE to pursue a 'boundaryless' culture where GE people were prepared to learn and grow across national and corporate boundaries. This was reinforced with the setting of demanding 'stretch' targets for performance and a compensation system that rewarded for corporate performance. In 1995, 22,000 staff at all levels held share options and had a clear financial incentive to pursue the corporate good.

In 1995, GE's businesses spanned over 100 countries generating sales of over $70 billion and net earnings of $6.5 billion. Against the previous year this represented a 17% increase in revenues, 11% increase in earnings and the twentieth year of increased dividends for shareholders.

Welch has spectacularly transformed the business. GE competes for victory today and for dominance in the future. It has laid out five mechanisms by which it will shape the future: globalisation, new products, information technology, service and quality. Welch looks ahead to a future where the cash-generating competitive machine he has created constantly renews itself to lead its markets and shape its future. Welch's personal beliefs, vision, mental power, toughness and charisma have created a business that is one of the best positioned to create and seize opportunities as we approach the millennium.

GAINING KNOWLEDGE AND INFORMATION (AGENDA ITEM ONE)

Your leadership responsibility is to gain knowledge and collect information to enable your people to gain an insight into tomorrow's opportunities. This information will allow you to decide how to lead your organisation to the future first. Such programmes for radical change fail for a number of reasons. These include:

- inadequate understanding of why the organisation should change and ineffective communication of why change is necessary
- lack of shared purpose, and inadequate sponsorship and senior commitment
- a poor strategy for implementing the change
- a lack of information to steer the change
- inadequate on-going and visible leadership.

The first step in introducing change is to gather the information necessary to articulate the case for change. In order to create the case for change you will need to draw together information and knowledge regarding: the macro-environment – the world around you; and the business itself, its rivals and its position. Chapters Two and Three explored this theme.

The case for change will be strong if:

- A critical aspect of the **macro-environment** is changing against the business. For example: economic downturn; worsening industrial relations affecting the cost and certainty of labour; government deregulation of the industry to allow easier entry.
- The organisation's position is weakening due to changes in the **industry**. For example: new entrants and existing competitors are competing for position; buyers are able to demand lower prices; new substitutes are being offered on better terms than the organisation's products.
- The **rivals** are stronger than the business in the markets, products, services, and processes where it matters and are determined to carry on winning. For example: new product introduction; entry into new markets; satisfaction of customers.

- The position is further weakening due to the organisation's presence in the wrong **market** segments. For example: the growing customer segments are ones where the business does not have product offerings; the value of products and services to customers has declined; others are introducing products that are better serving customer needs.
- The **suppliers** are becoming stronger than the business and this is likely to squeeze profits. For example: they are able to raise the price of their products; they supply rivals with components on better terms than the business; they are considering entering the industry through a foothold acquisition.
- The current **core strengths** are inadequate and are affecting the ability to compete. For example: some of the key products are unprofitable net of overhead costs; the coverage of channels and intermediaries is inadequate given the changes to consumer buying habits; the rate of innovation in introducing new products is far less than that of the nearest rivals.

With this knowledge you can formulate a compelling case for change. If yours is a strong case for change it will be life threatening, indisputable and close to happening. If well communicated, such a case can galvanise people to change. Your leadership responsibility is to ensure this happens.

One of the most effective communications of such a case that I have seen came from the managing director of a food business. He had a simple message: the parent had invested millions in technology and seen no return; their customer felt that his company's introduction of new products during the high season was too slow and lacked flair relative to rivals. As a result the company failed to maximise sales in this critical period; and their overheads were too high relative to rivals. This managing director gathered his directors and a hundred of the key opinion formers in his business around him and openly and honestly told them his diagnosis of the situation, his commitment to change and their role in making this change happen. This was the beginning of a highly effective and participative process of change.

DEVELOPING PURPOSE, STRATEGY AND TACTICS (AGENDA ITEM TWO)

Having identified the case for change you must galvanise your key people by developing a shared vision of the future and agreeing the strategy and tactics for achieving the vision. If the gap in your performance is vast the impact on the organisation will be dramatic, even transformational.

The first step in beginning a programme of change is to develop shared purpose. This section will focus on the key information required to develop a shared vision for transforming an organisation. It will also draw on the other sections of this book that describe the information required to develop the strategies and tactics and support a vision.

Figure 22 below presents KPMG's Change Management Globe.

Figure 22 *The Change Management Globe: an overall change framework*   **KPMG**

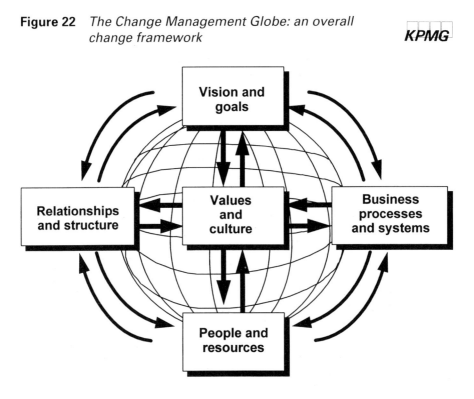

Vision and goals

What it wants to be in the future. Its goals are the targets it sets to achieve the vision.

The key information to find out is:

- what the current vision of the organisation's key decision-makers and influencers is and what their underlying goals are
- what the vision should be, given an understanding of the case for change – how you will shape the future of your industry
- what the critical success factors are and the few key things that need to be done well, and therefore
- where the organisation should focus its efforts
- what the resulting strategic and tactical plan of action should be.

Your responsibility is to lead your organisation to stretch itself and make a leap beyond the current boundaries of performance. The vision needs to be translated into a 'Mission-objective-success factor map'. The case of a major international credit-card company, in Figure 23 below, illustrates how such a map can be articulated and structured.

Figure 23   *Mission-objective-success factor map (example)*

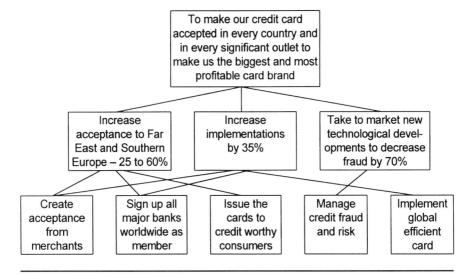

The implementation of the vision and goals requires strategies and tactics. Chapters Four and Five explored the information required to support the direction in which you wish to take the business. This was in the form of the following:

Attack, defence and retaliatory strategies
Based on the objective, determine:

- the attack strategy – the combination of frontal, flanking, encirclement, bypass and guerrilla attack that will enable victory
- the defence strategy – the combination of position, flanking, pre-emptive, counteroffensive, mobile and contraction defence that will enable the business to avoid defeat
- the retaliatory strategy to ensure that your rivals understand the organisation's commitment to the objective.

Tactical manoeuvres
Based on the strength of the current situation and objectives, determine:

- the moves that need to be made based on relative strengths and weaknesses
- the moves that need to be made to create and seize opportunities
- the readiness to act and react real time to seize initiative
- the signals and messages given to manipulate the enemy and keep the purpose and objectives secret.

The shared vision and goals will need to be underpinned by strategies and tactical plans of the type illustrated above. Once these have been formulated and agreed, the rest of the Change Management Globe can be used to develop the programme of change.

DEVELOPING THE PROGRAMME OF CHANGE (AGENDA ITEM THREE)

Having articulated the vision and goals, your next step is to develop the programme to deliver this change. Two themes have recently captured the imagination of the business world. They are corporate transformation, and business re-engineering or business process re-engineering (BPR). The two meet when BPR covers the whole organisation in a change that is radical, fundamental and seeks dramatic or transformational improvements in the business performance. However, whilst BPR focuses on transformation through *process* re-engineering, corporate transformation focuses on all aspects of change, including the strategy, the people, the processes, the products and services, the technology, the organisational structure and its values and cultures.

Corporate transformation

To achieve the vision the questions that need to be answered are:

- What processes and systems are needed?
- What products and services are needed?
- What people, resources and competencies are needed?
- How should these processes, people and resources be organised?
- What should the values and culture of the organisation be?
- What does the organisation currently look like?
- How far away from the vision is the organisation (gaps)?

The Change Management Globe (see Figure 22) will now be used to illustrate the information required to answer such questions and develop the programme of change. Figure 24 below gives a summary example of the before-and-after features of an organisation undergoing a corporate transformation programme.

Figure 24 *Corporate transformation programme*

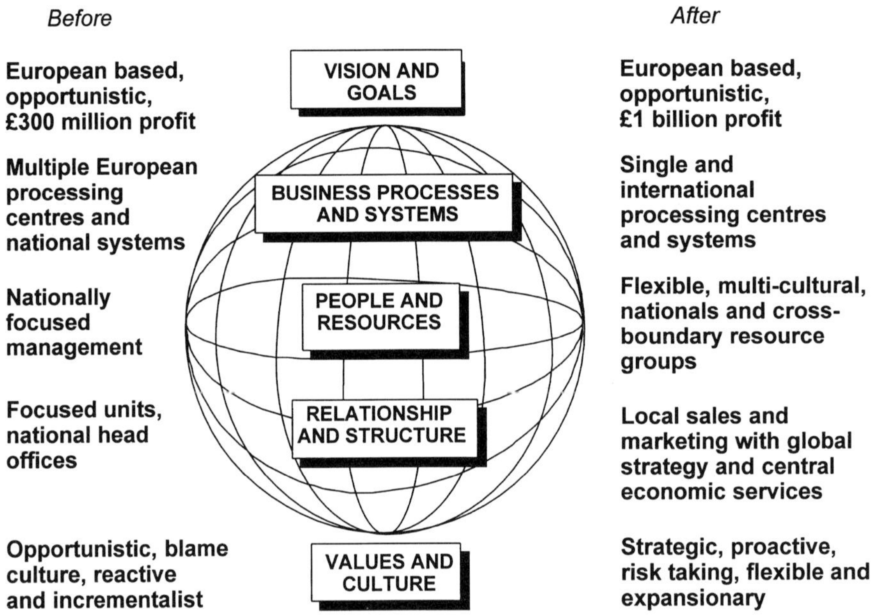

Before   *After*

European based,   VISION AND   European based,
opportunistic,   GOALS   opportunistic,
£300 million profit   £1 billion profit

Multiple European   Single and
processing   BUSINESS PROCESSES   international
centres and   AND SYSTEMS   processing centres
national systems   and systems

Nationally   Flexible, multi-cultural,
focused   PEOPLE AND   nationals and cross-
management   RESOURCES   boundary resource
                                             groups

Focused units,   RELATIONSHIP   Local sales and
national head   AND STRUCTURE   marketing with global
offices   strategy and central
                                             economic services

Opportunistic, blame   Strategic, proactive,
culture, reactive   VALUES AND   risk taking, flexible and
and incrementalist   CULTURE   expansionary

Business processes and systems

The cross-functional chain of activities and the technology and information systems needed to achieve the goals and vision.

Going clockwise around the Globe, the first assessment is of the business processes and systems and the products and services that go through these. Your leadership responsibility is to ensure that dramatic stretch targets are set to position your organisation to leap ahead in process performance.

The key information to find out is:

- what the link is between the key activities and processes of the organisation and its vision and goals
- how well current products and services meet customer needs and how well they flow through these processes to customers
- how well products, services and processes deliver value to the customer relative to those of rivals, in terms of cost, quality, volume, service, timing

- what the future products, services and processes should be to deliver the vision and goals
- how well systems and information support the delivery of value to customers
- what needs to change to achieve the vision and goals.

There are a number of examples of how processes have been transformed using technology. A typical example of re-engineering the sales and front-end sales order-taking process is provided in the case of Ascom Timeplex Inc, a telecommunications equipment business.

Ascom Timeplex Inc

Before
The old sales process was a paperchase involving securing sales leads from sales administration; requesting sales literature from marketing; getting quotes; typing proposals and faxing information to customers; getting information from the pricing, credit and manufacturing departments once the lead was firm; and, before placing the order, checking delivery dates with manufacturing.

After
Now when the company sends salespeople on a customer call they take a technology-packed laptop with them. The new re-engineered process provides laptop access to customer information prior to a visit; dialling into a worldwide network provides price lists, product information, and status reports on previous orders. Once the deal is struck the laptop records the order, vets for errors and transmits to head office for processing.

Source: J.W. Verity, 'Taking a laptop on a call' *Business Week*, 25 October 1993

The benefits of such programmes can be quantified in terms of cost, time to serve the customer, volume of business and quality of process. This section will also examine in more detail how process change can be designed and implemented.

People and resources

The human, technological, plant, brand and capital assets of the organisation, defined by the functionality they have and need to have.

Next, the people and resources of the organisation need to be assessed. The key information to find out is:

- what the inventory of the current supply of people and resources is
- what the gap in competency and capability between the required and current stock is
- what people and resources are needed to meet the demand from the business processes, organisation structure and relationships required in the future.

Table 9 *People and resources: ideas*

Resource characteristic	Current	Future
People	Many semi-skilled operatives with little authority, dealing with each other and limited functional responsibilities	Few skilled, trained and educated team workers, with wide, defined authority building customer relationships to provide services
Technological, plant and equipment	Fixed production specification supporting functional people, costly hardware, software and configuration, high maintenance cost, low information content	Flexible to design change, supporting processes, low cost easily configured, low maintenance needs, high information content
Brand	Long life, medium maintenance cost, high image content, manufacturer proprietary	Shorter life, high maintenance cost, high functionality content, customer-manufacturer owned
Capital	National, expensive, asset based	Global, competitively priced, floating across business

Table 9 above illustrates the type of ideas needed about the required future people and resources to realise the vision. The best source of such ideas is from some of the leading organisational specialists in the world and some of the examples set by existing companies, for example Semco, Sony and Hewlett Packard.

In the *Age of Unreason*, Charles Handy predicts: 'The new formula for success, and for effectiveness, is $I^3 = AV$, where I stands for Intelligence, Information and Ideas, and AV for added value in cash or in kind. In a competitive information society, brains on their own are not enough: they need good information to work with and ideas to build on if they are going to make value out of knowledge'.

Source: Charles Handy, *The Age of Unreason* (Business Books Ltd, 1989)

Relationships and structure

The way in which people and organisations interact with each other.

Continuing around the Globe, organisation structure and relationships now need to be assessed. The key information to find out is:

- what the current set of internal and external relationships are, for example between business units, with suppliers, customers, government
- how these are recognised within the formal structure and what the informal networks are
- what the impact of the networks on the vision, processes and people is
- what future relationships are required
- what needs to change to achieve these relationships and structures.

To support the transformed organisation a different type of organisation structure may be needed. The time taken to make the transition from the current state to some future networked or process-oriented organisation should not be underestimated. Figure 25 below illustrates the physical characteristics of such an organisation. Without the answer to the type of questions posed above such an organisation cannot be designed.

Figure 25   *Organisational change*

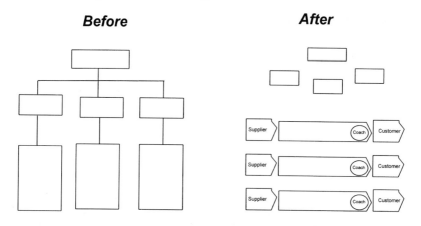

Vertical and hierarchical ... to... Horizontal and flat

Typical pros of vertical organisation   Typical cons of vertical organisation
- functional specialisation   - not organised to satisfy customers
- clear lines of authority   - bureaucratic and insular

In addition to the physical changes illustrated above, as organisational spread – geographic, hierarchical or functional – increases, informal networks gain in importance. The informal network of relationships is the key factor underpinning the formal organisation structure.

Pepsi-Cola International insists on the criticality of an 'informal matrix' cutting across functions, groups, people and disciplines. Jacobs Suchard, the Swiss confectioner, has a 'Euronetwork' of managers across European operations. Cadbury Schweppes, the UK food and drinks company, cites the benefit that 'building up informal links avoids organisational arthritis'. Wall Mart has invested in a private airline, video-conferencing and electronic messaging to build a network to pass learning across its US stores. The clear advantages enjoyed by these companies include:

- information creation and sharing
- stimulating innovation
- assisting the management of change
- facilitating problem-solving
- inducing cohesion, co-operation and synergy.

Most of these companies can point to tangible pay-offs in terms of the spread of best practice in areas such as stock management and customer service.

Values and culture

Prescribe 'how we do things around here'. The culture and values are formed from an organisation's past, its environment, its leaders and power groups. They are manifested in people's behaviour and assumptions which in turn reflect the underlying values of the organisation.

The final assessment of values and culture is perhaps one of the most critical if the vision to be achieved and the longer-term change is to be sustained. The key information to find out is:

- what diversity of talent you have and whether this is mobilised to construct potential new worlds or to compete against each other
- what the myths, legends, traditions and unwritten rules are
- what the current values and culture are
- what the values and culture required are to achieve the vision and goals
- what needs to change to establish a new set of values and behaviours.

The quest is to discover through the information collected just how much change is needed; how far the organisation has got in terms of changing; what the major areas of risk are; and what the barriers to successful change are. The result of these deliberations will allow the executive to introduce 'functional' projects, for example change location, change systems, change plant and equipment, and acquire different people to lead the organisation; and 'enabling' projects to create an environment for successful change, for example communication programmes, securing sponsorship, retraining and culture-change pro- grammes.

It is your leadership responsibility to create a winning culture that works with passion and pride to forge its own future.

Hewlett Packard

Hewlett Packard is renowned for the competitive advantage that its corporate culture gives it. Its culture, affectionately referred to internally as the 'HP Way', can be characterised by words such as innovation, quality, hardworking, fun, personal growth and devel- opment, caring and rewarding, risk-taking but safe products. HP works hard to create and maintain such a culture and value set. Its employees are paid in the top quartile in the locality and industry and are recruited according to whether employees will fit the HP Way; employees are provided with a wide range of classroom and on-the-job training including customer satisfaction and telephone answering skills; management by objectives includes personal as well as task objectives; management by wandering about is common in a high-productivity environment supported by one-per-desk PC- based workstations. Open communication of new product developments, sharing of profits and issuing of shares, performance-based reward, and open-plan, green, out-of-town sites are all essential features. This culture enables HP to rely on employees sharing risk – they take voluntary pay cuts when the company has financial concerns – staying non-unionised, being productive, ready and searching for change, and performing according to the strategy of the organisation.

Xerox

In 1993, Paul Allaire, chief executive officer and chairman, laid out a strategy to rejuvenate Xerox. One of the key elements of the strategy was to revamp Xerox's insular corporate culture by abandoning its 'go-it-alone' approach. A strong and commercial cultural message was given in its announcement of a partnership with Microsoft to market new lines of facsimile machines, photocopiers and printers – all of which are core business areas of Xerox.

Source: T. Smart, 'Can Xerox duplicate its glory days?' *Business Week*, 4 October 1993

The Change Management Globe (see Figure 22) illustrates the world of information required to create a programme that will transform an organisation. Success will of course only come from implementation of the functional and enabling projects to introduce change.

Business process re-engineering

One of the key dimensions of an organisation is its processes, the relative position of which is illustrated in the Change Management Globe. Process change is a key theme of the 1990s, and it will therefore be useful to explore the information required to create and implement such change.

Put simply, a business process is a series of related activities undertaken by a business to meet an objective. Business processes cut across functional boundaries and hierarchies. The end objective of a business process is to provide products or services to an external or internal customer.

Too many organisations only see business process re-engineering (BPR) as a tool for downsizing. When BPR is so narrowly perceived, it can have the adverse effect of downsizing the capability to compete effectively, shape the future, create new markets and offerings, and expand the business. If properly conducted, however, BPR can be of immense benefit.

Business process re-engineering is the action of introducing **radical** change, by addressing **fundamental** issues, that **cross functional boundaries**, in order to deliver **spectacular** benefits, through **combining** people, technology, structures and culture, which will transform **customer** focus.

This section will examine BPR across the spectrum of change from incremental improvement to a total rethink of the business, its relevance to the business and the information needed to use it. An overall approach to BPR is illustrated in Figure 26 below.

Figure 26   *Overall approach to business process re-engineering*

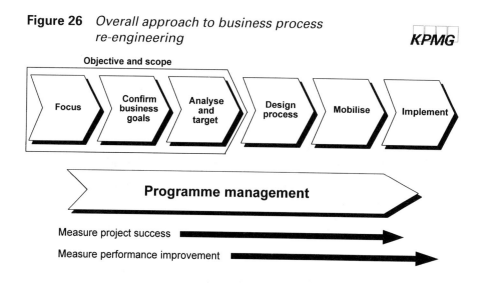

Objective and scope

Focus the programme
The programme for BPR should have a clear focus. The objective of the overall BPR programme and for each key business process should be defined in terms of the targeted scale of change; that is, is the organisation looking for incremental improvements, redesigning a few key processes or rethinking its approach to the market?

In order to answer this question, you must establish:

- the key business issues facing the organisation
- to what extent performance improvement is an issue
- to what extent processes are relevant to addressing these issues
- the other change programmes required to address remaining issues
- who the sponsors, advocates, change agents and targets are
- the likely future customer needs and the gap between current process capabilities and future requirements
- how well rivals' processes perform.

An important outcome is to build the business case for change based on the central business issues and an assessment of whether BPR is appropriate for addressing these issues. If BPR is appropriate, the objectives, scope, targets and sponsorship of the BPR programme should be agreed at the outset.

Figure 27 *Objective and scope – aspirational/stretch targets*

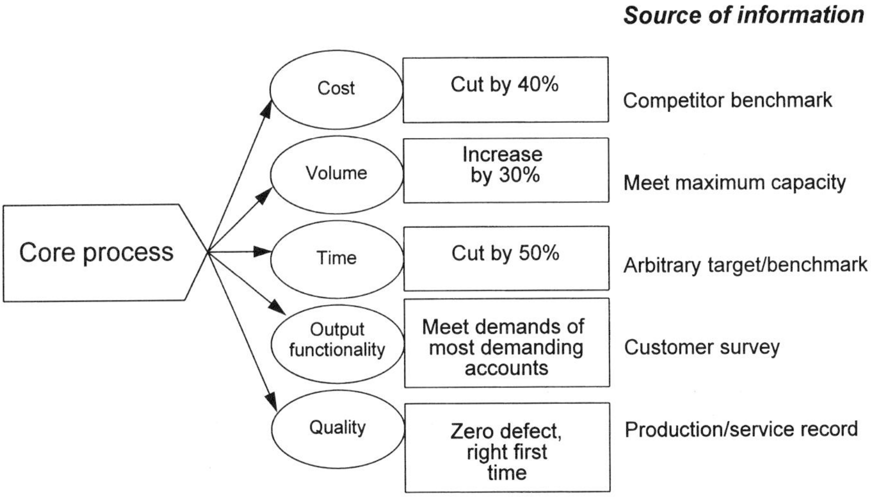

A structured approach is then required to achieve the benefits. Information technology (IT) is often used as a lever and enabler for achieving change. However, it is important to recognise that the imperatives for BPR could be strategic, IT-based, cultural or structural. Figure 27 above illustrates a suitable model for translating high-level statements into quantified objectives.

Business direction
The objective of this phase is to understand and articulate the strategic direction of the business. This will provide the context within which BPR will be carried out. The key information to find out is:

- what the clear statement of strategic intent or mission is
- what the objectives are underlying the statement
- what the key success factors are underlying each objective
- what the key business processes and functions are that contribute to success.

This high-level logical model is constructed at the senior management level and must be realistic, shared and measurable. The process of review involves challenging the underlying assumptions of the model through the type of information described in Chapters Two, Three and Four, and peer group and external challenge, for example from customers, suppliers and experts.

Analysis and targeting
The objective of this phase is to sufficiently analyse, review and work with the business and its customers and suppliers to understand the current performance, the potential future performance and the gaps. A high-level understanding is often sufficient in determining the redesign; too much information can often inhibit innovative design. The key information to find out is:

- what the products/services, activities, functions and processes are that are critical to achieving the targeted performance of the business

- what the attributes of the products/services, activities, functions and processes are, ie their costs, functionality, volume throughput, quality, speed, and their 'fit' to the market requirements – this will enable the organisation to focus its design efforts
- what the linkages between functions are in terms of the services provided by functions to each other to meet the external customer needs
- what the gaps are between the bottom-up model built up from the above three steps and the top-down, business direction-driven process view of the organisation that was developed with management
- for each key process whether the gaps in performance indicate the need for an incremental redesign or rethink.

Process design – designing your reposition

The objective of this phase is to identify and evaluate new ways of doing business in areas that most contribute to the goals of the organisation. For each process targeted for redesign, the company should have determined the approach based on the scale of targeted change, that is:

- For incremental improvement: the organisation needs to collect information to enable it to simplify the process by eliminating duplicate or redundant activities and rerouting other activities to improve efficiency.
- For redesigning business processes: the business needs to collect information to enable it to change the organisation of the process, the communication between units involved in the process, the use of IT, and the costs of the process.
- For radical rethinking: the organisation needs to collect information on potential future scenarios. These will need to be translated into objectives for the process and estimates of the value that the process is designed to deliver to customers. Its objective is to conceive new ways of satisfying those requirements without tying itself to what exists now.

It is important not to pigeon-hole opportunities too early on and to make the migration path between each of the above categories easy to traverse.

Regardless of how radical the repositioning, the information to find out is as follows:

- what are the outcomes required from the process to satisfy your customers' objectives?
- what activities need to be undertaken to deliver these outcomes?
- what is the best way to organise these activities?
- what linkages are required between functions and their activities?
- what reasons are required to fit the various roles, responsibilities, authority, skills and experience?
- what performance levels need to be achieved?

The example below provides an overview of the process re-engineering potential for a major food and drinks manufacturer. It has been greatly simplified to demonstrate the benefits.

Figure 28 below shows the transformation of a traditional functional organisation with strict demarcation of responsibilities between customers, sales order processing (Sales OP), logistics and factories. Each of the units has functional expertise, targets and systems.

To transform performance, the re-engineered scenario required:

- systems that support the process rather than the functions in their isolated routines
- EDI links between the customer and the company for speed and accuracy of transactions as well as facilitating the relationship
- a shared database to understand the full extent of the business with the customer and enable cross-selling opportunities to be exploited
- greater skills in the factory
- elimination of duplicate or unnecessary activities
- process-performance targets rather than just functional ones.

Figure 28 *Process re-engineering (example)*

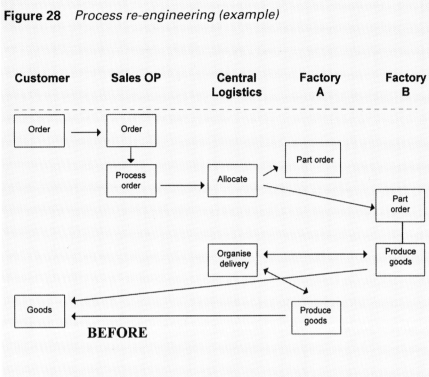

Mobilisation

Mobilising resources is the first step in implementation. Whether to go for a piloting (ie testing the solution by implementing in one part of the organisation) or a 'big bang' (ie fully implementing all the changes) approach depends on:

- whether an incremental, redesign or rethink solution is to be implemented
- the existing level of organisational commitment to the change being introduced
- the certainty of the management team in the validity of the redesign
- the risk-return trade-off that the management team is willing to make – implementation without piloting is a risky option but has a faster return than with piloting
- the track record of management in managing change and specifically the skills and experience in the areas of change envisaged.

Implement new business designs

The effort required to implement depends on the degree of change to be introduced, and therefore the work to be undertaken in this stage cannot be prescribed. However, the potential implications of implementation, which should not be underestimated, include:

- large-scale redundancies, including delayering of management as well as elimination of redundant activities
- outsourcing of activities that are not strategic and not a core competence and for which there exists an efficient external market
- organisational change from changing functional boundaries, responsibilities and groupings
- senior management change, including the replacement of some senior managers
- change from dominance of functional vertical hierarchy to horizontal management in some key business processes
- development of new competencies and capabilities including retraining of large sections of the organisation in new methods, working practices and skills

- implementation of systems to enable the performance improvement.

The implementation programme has the following elements:

- specifying and managing the human dimension of the change, and
- specifying and managing the individual 'physical' change projects to achieve the process redesigns – the success criteria have already been defined and implementation success should be measured on the basis of achieving these criteria.

As you can see, information plays a key part in undertaking BPR. Knowledge of our organisation, our relative competitive position, and the levers of change is critical to creating solutions, which may range from the incremental to the transformational. Success comes from **delivering** improvements in performance. For a constant willingness to change, a knowledge-based organisation, with the implied understanding of its position, is likely to be able to re-engineer with greater ease than one that works in ignorance of its position.

DEVELOPING THE INFORMATION TO MONITOR AND FUEL CHANGE (AGENDA ITEM FOUR)

Having established the programme of change that will deliver the vision and goal of the organisation, the decision-makers need to be fed with information so that they can monitor and steer the necessary course. This section will examine the principles and building blocks of such an information system and provide some frameworks for creating it. The steps will be to:

- establish the importance of creating a picture of the world that changes as the world changes – a 'moving picture'

- highlight the need for 'hard' as well as 'soft' information
- describe what information is needed
- describe who the organisation should compare itself to
- provide some frameworks for how to draw all this information together.

Your leadership responsibility is to ensure that your organisation, ahead of your rivals, has the best view of the likely future of your industry and the implications for your markets. As a result, you will be best placed to profit from the industry outcome.

The moving picture

Snap shots

A critical aspect of competing to profit from future outcomes is developing a moving picture of potential opportunities. Most companies take monthly snap shots of a small part of the world around them to make decisions, which has been demonstrated to be woefully inadequate. This section will briefly examine the importance of the moving picture and the information required to create one.

During the first half of 1993, the Metropolitan Police in London advertised on the London Underground train network to illustrate the complexity, depth and breadth of the job facing them. One advert in particular illustrated the importance of the moving picture. A snap shot showed a casually dressed black man running fast on a high street; in hot pursuit was a white police officer. The poster asked if we assumed that the black man was a criminal being chased by the police. In fact, he was a plain-clothes police officer who, together with his uniformed white colleague, was chasing a third man outside the frame of the snap shot. This graphically illustrates the dilemma faced in making decisions based on a partial and static picture of the world.

In the context of corporate information systems, what information will provide a moving picture? Today's technologies do not permit an organisation to have a moving picture at its finger tips; it is unlikely that there will ever be information available of the 'omniscient' type.

However, through a collection of snap shots it may be possible to gather a bigger picture of what is happening. An example of the series of snap shots that could be compiled is outlined below.

Customers
Customers can tell the organisation directly or through third-party market researchers:

- the fit between the organisation's products and approach and their needs
- the advantages and disadvantages of the organis-ation's products relative to rivals'
- their future requirements.

Customer-facing people
- marketing people can tell the organisation what the consumers think of its products relative to its rivals
- the front-line sales force can tell the organisation what its customers think of its products and approach to them relative to the organisation's rivals
- servicing and maintenance people can tell the organisation what customers think of the reliability of its products and their longer-term relevance to their business
- telephone support people can tell the organisation about the types of problems that its customers experience.

In-house functions and process people
- finance people can tell the business about the cost of its activities, the profitability of its products, customer relationships and market segments, regions and channels and the prima facie reasons for variances in revenue, profits and costs
- production people can tell the business about the ease of manufacture using its technology, the timeliness of the information received from sales, or logistics on what to produce
- marketing people can tell the business about the match between produced products and customer demand.

Systems
- financial systems can show the business the match between actual costs and budgets and the variances
- the production system can show the business the adherence of its production to volume, schedule and cost targets and size of inventory
- the distribution system can show how often the distribution function matches customer-delivery requirements in terms of product delivered on time and schedule.

Brokers and the media
- the media can tell an organisation what its rivals say about themselves and the business
- brokers can tell an organisation what value they place on its actions and talk in terms of the value of the company.

Stakeholders
- the Government can tell the business what it thinks of the future state of the economy, and the industry's importance in political and economic terms
- the regulator can tell the business how he intends to change the structure of the industry and its profitability
- the shareholders can tell the business whether they are happy or unhappy with its decisions, performance and the future returns profile.

These examples are not exhaustive, but serve to illustrate the quite detailed and diverse information that can be collected.

Collecting changing information
These snapshots become a moving picture if information is gathered when it changes significantly. For example:

- customer information could be collected quarterly and on the introduction of new product or approaches to the market
- information from front-line people could be collected monthly to highlight changes to a quarterly detailed picture

- information from internal people could be collected weekly, monthly or quarterly and by exception on an 'as it happens' basis for major changes
- systems information could be on a similar cycle
- information from brokers and the media could be collected 'as it happens'
- information from stakeholders could be on a half-yearly basis and by exception on an as it happens basis for major changes.

The moving picture requires an information machine to be created to systematically collect, filter, process, analyse, format and deliver information to the relevant decision-makers, influencers and controllers.

How good is the picture that has been developed?

One thing to bear in mind is that a computer's intelligence can be no greater than that of the people who programme and use it, which may severely handicap the machine. The *quality* of the moving picture will need to be judged before it can be used to make decisions. The key factors determining quality are given below:

- Can it be confirmed from an independent perspective?
- Is there any contradictory evidence?
- Is it based on information collected over a reasonable time span or does it concentrate on one period?
- Is it biased by the researcher's preferences?
- Has research been challenged and corroborated?
- Has it been checked for accuracy, sufficiency, stability and relevance?
- Is judgement clearly separated from empirical evidence?
- Is the picture complete?
- How does it compare to other pictures – the organisation's and others'?
- Does the picture focus attention on critical issues or does it attach equal weight to all matters?

A major issue for management is the use of the existing information before further investments are made. Various database marketing techniques and tools are available to allow the organisation to exploit its information.

In this way it can improve performance and better penetrate existing customers with existing or new products. Neural networks (see below), knowledge-based systems and statistical models are also available to assist the company to better exploit the information.

Neural networks

Neural networks, a much promised breakthrough from the information scientists, are beginning to have some small success in narrower commercial applications. A neural network is a 'trained' model which, based on understanding inputs and outputs from a series of examples, accepts new inputs to produce or predict the outcome.

Direct marketing: an insurer selling personal loans

The problem
The motor insurance division of a company with a database of 3 million customers wants to sell a new loan product. It test-markets its loan-offering to a random sample of 75,000 customers and achieves a 2% response rate of 1,500.

The neural model
The company uses a neural network to analyse the application forms returned and build a predictive neural model. The application forms have captured personal information on the respondents such as age, sex, address, occupation, loyalty (time as customer), and scope (number of policies held). The neural network model is fed with the whole 75,000 customers indicating the 1,500 that had responded. The model scores the customers with a 'likely response rate' and indicates that most respondents are male, aged 25 to 40, C1 socio-economic class and come from the west and north of the country. Traditional statistical methods could reveal such a result. However, the neural network likely response rate provides a probability based on a combination of factors.

The application and the benefits
The result is applied to the database of customers and 500,000 out of 3 million customers are mailed. The response rate is 5%: 25,000 positive responses. This more than halves the cost of the direct marketing programme. The disadvantages of such a model are that it is not self-explanatory, it is not apparent how this likely response rate has been calculated and training is slow.

Monitoring progress and managing change

In managing the change programmes introduced to transform a corporation or its processes, the hard needs to be combined with the soft. The hard is the quantitative assessment of the progress to time and schedule and the soft is the qualitative assessment of the progress in changing people's values and beliefs to build the commitment.

The **hard** information to collect concerns:

- The progress of the 'functional' change projects, in terms of adherence to deadlines and achievement of milestones. It is important to measure progress of the programme's completion; however, too many change projects focus *only* on the completion of the programme. They define their success criteria in terms of the number of people trained, the hours expended and the money spent.
- The size and rate of delivery of performance improvements. The measurement of performance improvements delivered is essential to achieve a transformed organisation. Hard measurements of costs reduced, volume increased, product quality improved and cycle time reduced are all important.
- The efficiency and effectiveness of the ongoing management of the business. This can be measured using a combination of internal and external measures.

The **soft** information to collect is:

- The extent to which there is reduced commitment to the status quo. This involves identifying whether the organisation has understood what is wrong with the current situation and explaining to its people the painful implications of not changing.
- The extent to which commitment has been generated to the future situation that is trying to be achieved. The organisation needs to ascertain whether it has helped people understand what the future means for *them* and how they fit into it.

- The political and emotional considerations in making the decision. The business needs to understand who supports it, who is against it and who fears the change.
- The effectiveness of sponsors in demonstrating commitment, resolve and leadership.
- The extent of resistance to the change process.
- The effectiveness of advocates and change agents.
- The effectiveness in generating congruent behaviour between groups with common objectives.

Benchmarking

One of the key tools to help an organisation learn about how well it is performing and to provoke change is benchmarking. As the leader you must ensure that your organisation learns from its experiences and from others.

What should you compare?

If an organisation's managers do not focus on the right things to benchmark and then take action to change, they will simply be 'industrial tourists' rather than strategists seeking to build on successful practices and learn from the success of others. Comparisons should be made of:

- strategy
- tactical manoeuvres
- core operations and functions
- processes and activities.

Strategy

An organisation's strategy is evident from the market share it gains, the profits it makes, the growth of its business, the cost of operating, its marketing situation, the satisfaction of its customers, and its rate of innovation.

Benchmarks of strategy include comparison of:

- External financials – market share, profit, growth of products, and their performance within the market segments and geographic areas in which the organisation competes. This information will encourage the business to focus on specific products, segments or geographic areas.

- Internal financials – cost structure split simply in terms of cost of sales, other direct costs and support costs. This will encourage an organisation to examine the cost of its operations, functions and processes, and productivity in terms of sales or output per person. This will then encourage the business to examine the organisation of its operations and processes.
- Marketing stance – marketing mix (promotions, prices and places) of products in each market segment against the previous information on share, profit and growth. This will encourage an examination of the tactics adopted in each segment.
- Customer satisfaction with products. This will encourage the organisation to focus on specific products and customers, and the processes by which the products are delivered to the customers.
- Innovation: rate of innovation or development and introduction of new products or applications. This will encourage an examination of the processes underlying research and development.

Such benchmarks should provide an organisation with an indication of the results of its strategy and where to focus its more detailed benchmarking efforts.

Tactical manoeuvres
Remembering Clausewitz's definition that 'Tactics is the art of using troops in battle', a distinction is made here between the battle scenario and the business-as-usual scenario. The latter will be referred to as core operations and functions. It is one removed from the battle and although it contributes to the winning and losing of battles it is not part of the specific moves made in the short term to influence an outcome.

Benchmarks are required of the impact during tactical manoeuvres of the following:

- for short-term changes in price, promotion, product attributes and place, the change in market share and profitability impact on costs and profits

- for short-term alliances with suppliers or buyers, the impact on market share and profitability
- for introductions of variations to existing products or services, the impact on market share and profitability.

Such benchmarks should provide an estimate of the impact of tactics and the *potential* benefits of various tactics in terms of the sensitivity of market share and profits to changes in marketing mix, alliance and new products.

Core operations and functions
Benchmarks of operations and functions include comparison of operations such as manufacturing, sales and distribution, and other functional support units such as finance and procurement.

The comparisons should be of:

- productivity
- throughput, cycle time and quality measures
- stock levels
- headcount
- overheads as a proportion of direct cost
- cost.

Such benchmarks should provide an estimate of *potential* operating size and efficiency.

Processes and activities
The comparisons should be of:

- customer performance measures, for example adherence to schedule, timeliness and customer service
- internal process performance measures, for example throughput, cycle time and quality measures, headcount and cost
- activity-based performance measures, such as activity cost and cost per unit of cost driver, for example procurement cost per order, or PC support cost per PC user.

Figure 29 below presents an illustration of the benchmarks of internal and external information and the implications for performance improvement. The information provided is as follows:

- The 'dimensions' of the business, for example its products, customers, regions, distribution channels, market segments and strategic business units. These dimensions define the complexity of the business and the likely complexity of its value chain.
- The profitability of the business along each of its dimensions, for example the profitability of each of its products. This requires information to be gathered on the costs and revenues attributable to each unit in a dimension, for example the costs and revenues of each product.

Figure 29 *Multi-dimensional profitability*

These dimensions are key drivers of profitability and give clear internal 'benchmarks' as a basis for performance improvement.

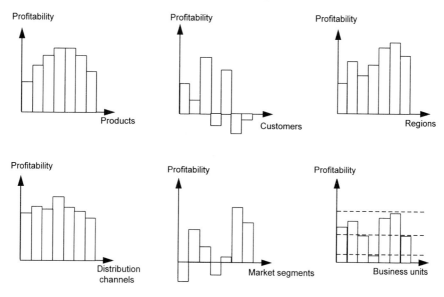

Figure 30 below illustrates how management attention can be focused by:

- Selecting dimensions that will have the greatest impact on the business. In Figure 30 these are the products, customers, distribution channels and business units.
- The comparison of profitability of individual elements, for example the least profitable products, customer relationships, channels and business units.

Figure 30   *Information to focus management attention*

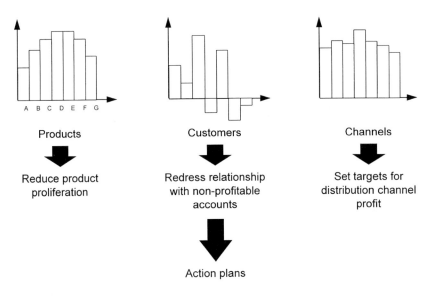

Profitability information is provided to focus management attention on specific areas. Internal action plans are developed to achieve improved performance.

A radically simpler set of benchmarks for 'forecasting victory or defeat' is provided below.

'Therefore, in your deliberations, when seeking to determine the military conditions, let them be made the basis of a comparison, in this wise.

(1)   Which of the two sovereigns is imbued with the moral law?
(2)   Which of the two generals has the most ability?
(3)   With whom lie the advantages derived from Heaven and Earth?
(4)   On which side is discipline most rigorously enforced?
(5)   Which army is the stronger?
(6)   On which side are the officers and men more highly trained?
(7)   In which army is there greater constancy both in reward and punishment?'

(Sun Tzu)

The five constant factors underlying these comparisons can be equated in terms of the corporate context as follows:

(1)   **'The moral law'** – personal power and influence or corporate culture
(2)   **'Heaven'** – the macro-level environment and other exogenous factors
(3)   **'Earth'** – the nature of the market
(4)   **'The commander'** – the leader
(5)   **'Method and discipline'** – organisation, structure, process, channels, logistics and control.

Who should you compare yourself to?

We should learn from those that are better than us, and ideally from those that are the best. Recognising *what* we want to learn, we are better able to determine from *whom.* The benchmarks will be those best at strategy, best at tactics, best at specific operations and functional management and those best at processes and activities. The peers to compare yourself with are:

- **Rivals**, especially on strategy, tactics and industry-specific operations and processes.
- **'Best of breed.'** In this case, non-industry specific operations are being compared, for example distribution; functions, for example finance; and non-industry specific processes and activities.

- **Internal best performers**. This comparison would be across a portfolio of similar units, for example a bank may compare its branches, a power company its power stations, a retail chain its high-street shops, the National Health Service its hospitals.

How should the information be structured?

It is difficult to acquire a broad and complex set of data; most of the information on benchmarking is too high level and therefore not actionable. However, a combination of desk and field research can provide an array of valuable facts.

The resulting benchmarks need to be combined in a balanced way to focus on the few key factors which will influence strategic objectives. A suitable management tool, an executive dashboard, is required, an example of which is the **Business Balanced Scorecard**.

With the right measures of performance a strategy can be reinforced through giving feedback or reward, and learning lessons from success or failure. If performance is not adequately measured, an organisation's strategies will become show-pieces of its intellectual intent but not its implementation intent. This seems obvious, yet as KPMG's Harris survey research shows (see pp 12–13), companies set grand statements of their vision, articulate their objectives and critical success factors, state in hallowed, well-researched documents the forces determining the nature of their industries and their core competencies – and then continue to use the same short-term financial indicators that they have always used. Measures such as return on capital employed, trading profit, and profit before interest and tax will not measure the performance of the business in achieving new strategies nor will they encourage new behaviour. Such measures may well be the final outcome of the strategies but will not tell an organisation whether its strategies are working or not.

It is right not to abandon financial measures, but these need to be combined with the non-financial measures and with external measures of performance.

What is the Business Balanced Scorecard?

The Business Balanced Scorecard is a tool for articulating strategy and measuring performance. It was developed by Professor Robert S. Kaplan and David Norton and first proposed in 'The Balanced Scorecard – measures that drive performance', *Harvard Business Review*, January–February 1992.

Figure 31 below demonstrates the Business Balanced Scorecard. A key point to note about the Scorecard is its alternative perspectives – those of the customer, process, stakeholder, and innovation and learning. Another point to note is the balanced nature of the Scorecard. It requires an organisation to balance the ambitions implicit in its vision and, by identifying the underlying success factors and deliverables, to consider whether they are realistic. So, for example, is it possible to be the lowest-cost producer whilst producing the highest functionality products tailored to every individual market segment? Is this the new reality of competition that is achievable and will deliver market dominance or is the business deluding itself? And should it realistically expect the market to polarise into those who want functionality tailored to their needs and are prepared to pay premium prices for it, and those who want basic products at bargain prices? Management must form their view and balance their Scorecard.

The strategic planning process involves the articulation of the vision of a business, the identification of the key objectives that underlie the vision, and the few things that need to be done well to achieve the key objectives. The Business Balanced Scorecard provides the measures that tell the organisation whether it is successfully improving its performance.

Figure 31   *The Business Balanced Scorecard*

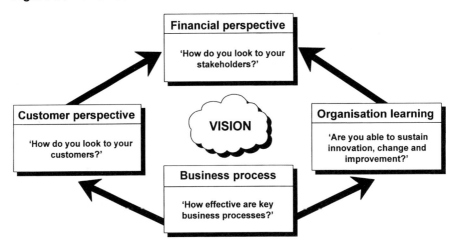

**The Business Balanced Scorecard at this point ensures a coherent
package of business performance measures and proves the
consistency of the vision and goals.**

Why are tools such as the Scorecard important?

Having set the strategy and explored the implications in the
logical model explained above, the business can be steered
using the Scorecard measures. For the Scorecard to be a
reality, it needs to be linked into the actions of the business.
The customer perspective provides a focal point for the
organisation's processes. These processes need to be
efficient and designed to deliver value to the organisation's
customers. The ability to innovate and grow determines
the ability to continue to meet customer demands.
Although cost management is essential, if the business
gets the other perspectives right the financial results will
follow.

If the Scorecard is too difficult to deliver to the desks of
executives, it will soon be abandoned. A common
complaint regarding conventional information systems
and reports is 'Too much data, not enough information'.
The plethora of unreconciled systems that tell an
organisation how it is performing in all the areas of the
business and fail to highlight the key pieces of information
that should be actioned, can be rationalised and structured
using the Scorecard. The Scorecard can represent the top

window into the company's information systems – the 'Executive Information System' (EIS). The EIS would be linked to the key information systems, which in turn pull data from the core business/operational systems. This hierarchy of information can be used to enable drill-down into the transactional data to answer questions of performance asked at the top level by the executives.

How to use the Scorecard

The Business Balanced Scorecard is a simple management tool. Such tools must enable senior management to focus on the key aspects of the business to meet their vision. Figure 32 below provides an example of the use of the Business Balanced Scorecard.

Figure 32 *Using the Business Balanced Scorecard (example)*

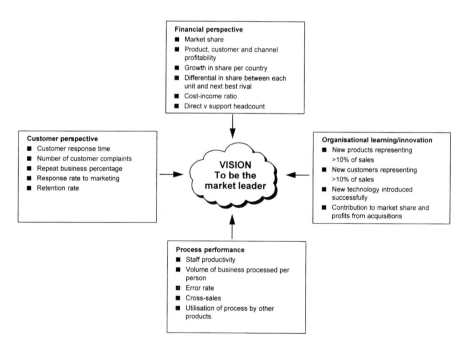

(Adapted from R.S. Kaplan and D. Norton, 'The Balanced Scorecard – measures that drive performance'.)

The Scorecard is a useful tool because it provides:

- A framework for articulating strategy. The Scorecard requires that the vision of the organisation be properly articulated and balanced. The vision has to be expressed in terms of the four dimensions of stakeholder, customer, process and organisational learning. Conflicting priorities across these dimensions need to be resolved.
- A means for measuring and reviewing performance. The Scorecard at the top level allows executives to review the performance of the business along the key dimensions.
- Structuring of information collected. It allows the information collected by the organisation to be structured in accordance with the dimension and measure it supports. This process alone highlights the inadequacy of current information collected and the gaps in the information currently provided.
- A framework for determining the role of systems in meeting strategic objectives. It allows the organisation's systems to be seen in the light of the executives' view of what is important for the business to achieve. The overall role of the systems in providing value to the vision becomes clearer by addressing which systems support the customers, which the processes, which the organisation's innovation and which the stakeholder.

As a strategic tool the Scorecard can be used to:

- build up a picture of the performance measures of rivals
- benchmark performance against peers
- explore alternative performance scenarios.

The Scorecard is not the answer to all performance measurement problems: it provides a means of articulating, testing and monitoring performance. However, it is not designed to measure:

- the success of tactical moves
- the success of attack, defence and retaliatory strategies
- detailed progress in the delivery of a corporate transformation or business process re-engineering programme

- the impact of changes in the environment or structure of the industry, in the way that, say, Porter's industry-structure analysis (see pp 70–72) does.

To expect one tool to capture all of this is unrealistic. The Business Balanced Scorecard is a key tool during the strategic planning process and for keeping the score once the strategy has been determined. It does *not* negate the need to use other strategy formulation tools and information systems.

To widen the relevance of management tools such as the Business Balanced Scorecard, the following section examines the use of a construct called the Corporate Knowledge Base.

Figure 33   *The Corporate Knowledge Base*

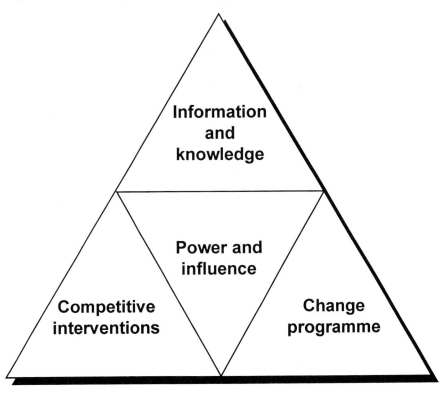

The Corporate Knowledge Base

To be in the strongest position to utilise the information that will enable an organisation to create strategic advantage, it needs an information system that brings together the key themes explored in this book. The framework of such a system, the Corporate Knowledge Base (CKB), is illustrated in Figure 33 above.

The CKB brings together the information required for an organisation to assess the world around it and determine its course of action. It is based on an assessment of the following:

Power and influence

This comprises an assessment of current and future:

- holders of power who initiate and sustain change of a physical or attitudinal nature
- holders of influence who determine the nature and course of the change
- the relationships between these power bases.

Information and knowledge

The three key elements that provide the knowledge to exercise power and enable strategy, planning and action are an assessment of current and future:

- strengths and weaknesses
- competitors and suppliers
- position in the industry, market and in the eyes of customers.

Competitive interventions

This comprises an assessment of the current and future impact of:

- attack strategies
- defence strategies
- retaliatory strategies
- tactical manoeuvres.

The outcomes of change programmes

This comprises an assessment of the results of current and future:

- vision and goals in securing clarity, unity and satisfying stakeholders, for example through providing commensurate financial results
- product and service innovations and their ability to meet current and future customer needs
- projects to create effective processes and systems
- development of people and resources to create core competencies
- efforts to strengthen and create new external and internal relationships
- changes to structure to improve the ability of managers and people to compete and manage
- projects to create a constructive and winning culture and set of values.

Such information will help address the success of management of change. The detailed information supporting the CKB will allow strategy units to analyse and interpret the actions of the company in meeting the agenda.

Decision-provoking and decision-taking

The role of the analyst and adviser

The information presented in the Corporate Knowledge Base allows decisions to be made in the knowledge of the relevant changes in the world. A typical business day is taken up by a plethora of decisions as a matter of routine ranging from the strategic to the operational. Much of the information received has been sent without any foresight and without any proactive indication of what should be done with it. However, the clever analysis and presentation of such information enables the information analysts and advisers to *provoke* decisions. An illustration of decision-provoking information is given below.

Decision-provoking

Taking into account the information thesis presented in this book, decision-provoking information includes asking questions in the format, '**Did you know ... unless we respond?**' For example:

- The Government is about to change its policy on X (the industry, product, environment, trade, interest rates, etc) which will damage profitability by Y.
- Customers are increasing their demands in the area of X (prices, functionality, time, innovation, schedule adherence, etc) which will result in a decrease in our turnover by Y.
- We have spent £X million on competitive strategies (attack, defence or retaliation) across the European region. However, the return from this in market share terms is X% and only £Y million in terms of improvement to profits. This will damage future credibility in the market.
- Rivals are about to undertake competitive move X (cut prices, introduce new product, distribute through new channels, etc) which will damage market share by Y.
- X of the top 10 (products, major accounts, branches, channels, etc) are not profitable after the attribution of relevant overhead support costs by Y.
- Key business process W (claims processing, order fulfilment, new product introduction, etc) is being outperformed (cost, volume throughput, cycle time, customer-service response, etc) by the best of breed peer by a factor of X and is estimated to be below the achievable re-engineered potential by a factor of Y. This will damage our ability to retain customers and will lose us a Z% share of new business.

Deciding for yourself – the responsibility of the leader

The type of clear case for change illustrated above is likely to provoke decisions. The key elements are the need to: present to the decision-makers a matter of critical importance; quantify the impact on the organisation's performance (wherever possible, this should be converted into the impact on the company's profit, market share or sales, and therefore the impact of inaction); and knock a long-held belief.

Executives need to examine such information with caution. They need to ask themselves, 'What bias has been given to the information on which I am to base my decisions?', 'What specious alternatives are being set up to show the analyst's preferred option in a favourable light?', 'What am I not being told that makes this information look so clear cut?' and 'How shall I challenge and test it?'

The analysis and interpretation provided by analysts and advisers needs to be combined with a judicious review of the core information supporting the Corporate Knowledge Base to allow a view to be formed and to judge how change should be created and managed.

DEVELOPING SELF (AGENDA ITEM FIVE)

The qualities and attributes of the leader have been explored in each chapter of this book. You have been encouraged to assess yourself if you are really to make a difference to your organisation's position. It has been shown that the responsibility of the leader is to the people he leads, the customers, suppliers and other stakeholders. It should be added that the leader also has a responsibility to himself and to his family. Leadership is not a role to be taken lightly.

Taking the decision to initiate and manage change requires the rational, political and emotional considerations to be weighed up. Information is the common ingredient to feed these decision-making factors. It is not sufficient just to provide the 'hard' or rational information; the 'soft' information is also required. There is a need to be able to understand the mindset of each of the protagonists in the game. The motivations, assumptions, commitments, potential and ambitions of each protagonist need to be well understood to enable the business to determine the moves it wishes to make and predict the likely retaliations and countermoves.

Such evaluations need to fit within the context of under-standing self. The purpose of this book is not to lead such an exploration: the understanding and development of self is a life-long journey and one that would be futile to explore within such narrow confines.

However, this book does encourage an exploration of needs, motives, determinations and capabilities. The questions to answer are:

- What do you want?
- Why do you want it?
- How badly do you want it?
- Are you capable of getting what you want?
- What is your purpose?

The determination of purpose is a critical personal milestone in the journey of self-exploration. Of course, this purpose will change over time. In its spiritual sense the self may never be fathomed. In the simpler context of the use of information in business, executives need to ensure that they have arrived at a purpose that is worthy of them, their people and organisation and is sufficiently long term and challenging to be a mission. If information systems are well developed, the information needed will be acquired; if their self is well developed and renewed in accordance with the changes around them, they will be able to better lead their people and organisation. Undertaking an exploration to gain awareness will enable you to better achieve the following:

Assess the situation
- assess the situation with clarity and within the wider context
- assess how the situation will change with clarity.

Develop vision
- clearly develop a vision of where the world is going
- clearly develop a vision of where the world could go.

Develop mission
- clearly develop a mission for yourself
- chart a course for how you will get there.

Read your rivals
- assess your rival's self – including his motivations, assumptions, commitments, potential and ambitions
- assess your rival's likely moves – attacks, defences and retaliations.

Lead your people
- motivate, unite and lead your people
- coach and develop your people.

Steer your organisation
- make your organisation ready and prepared for change
- change its route in accordance with circumstance.

The exploration of self is a critical element in the making of the master strategist who is described in Chapter One as:

'that unique person who is better able to assimilate knowledge than his opponents and thereby forms superior strategies'.

*IN THIS CHAPTER*_____

The key themes of this book were drawn together to demonstrate how to manage and create your agenda for change. The model of omniscience laid out in Chapter One was extended to explore the information that is needed to establish the case for changing an organisation. This case is the basis of mobilising an organisation behind a vision of the future and the strategies and tactics required to deliver the vision.

The creation of unity of purpose is the first step in articulating the programme of change. KPMG's Change Management Globe was used as the means of defining the current and future state of the organisation and to develop the change programme. We then focused on the information required to manage and deliver changes to an organisation's processes.

The aim of such information is to monitor and fuel change. Benchmarking information was seen as an important tool for assessing performance relative to internal and external peers. The Business Balanced Scorecard was examined as a way of capturing a balanced view of performance and it was shown how a powerful information system, the Corporate Knowledge Base, could draw together information and knowledge of the outside world, competitive interventions and programmes to change the business.

One of the key themes running through the book is the central and critical role of the leader: we recognised that to manage and lead change requires visionary and purposeful leadership. This chapter ended by touching on the importance of assessing, developing and renewing yourself in order to enable you to better lead yourselves and your organisations. The principles of the chapter are illustrated in Figure 34 below.

'If you know the enemy and know yourself, your victory will not stand in doubt; if you know Heaven and know Earth, you may make your victory complete.'

Sun Tzu, *The Art of War*

Figure 34 *Executive decision-making: creating and managing change*

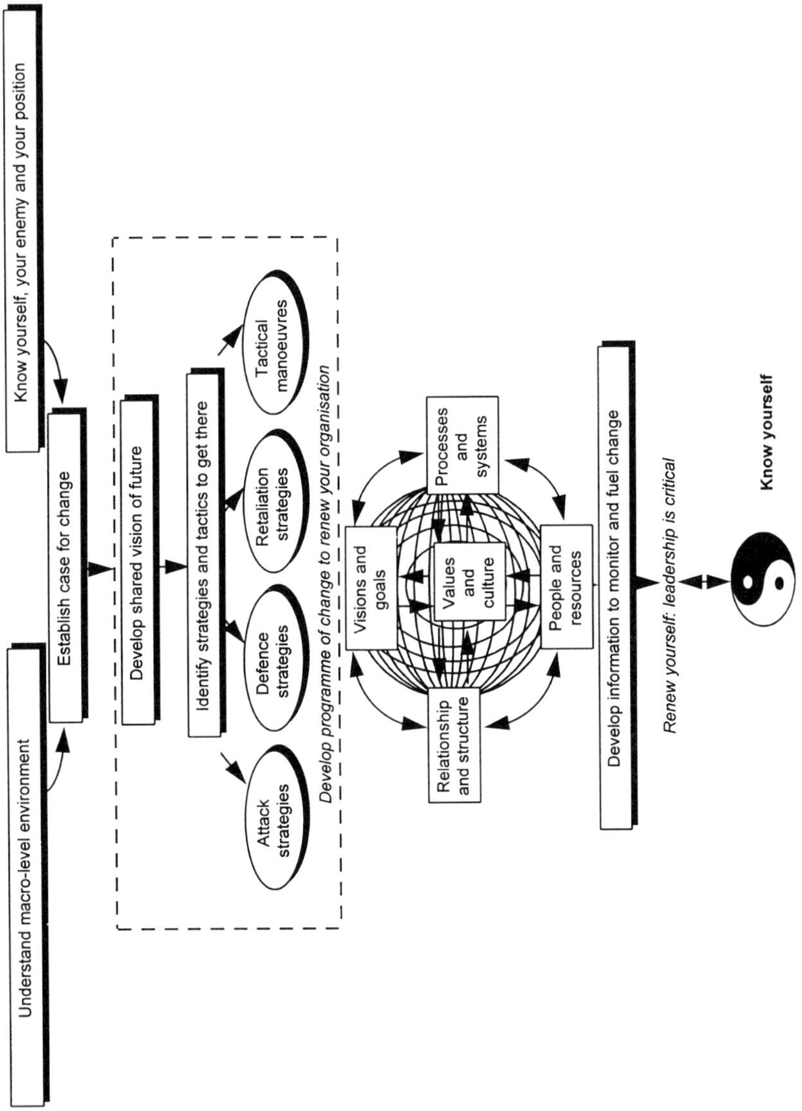

Know yourself, your enemy and your position

Understand macro-level environment

Establish case for change

Develop shared vision of future

Identify strategies and tactics to get there

Tactical manoeuvres

Retaliation strategies

Defence strategies

Attack strategies

Develop programme of change to renew your organisation

Visions and goals

Values and culture

Processes and systems

People and resources

Relationship and structure

Develop information to monitor and fuel change

Renew yourself: leadership is critical

Know yourself

Appendix

FORMULATING STRATEGIC OPTIONS*

* The type of strategic analysis illustrated in this Appendix is fast becoming a
commodity in today's business environment. Indeed, those that can't achieve
this level of analysis and thought will soon be unable to compete at all: any
success they may have will be transitory and accidental.

ILLUSTRATION 1:
COMBINING INTERNAL AND EXTERNAL INFORMATION

This illustration provides a description of the analysis required to combine internal and external factors and identify and evaluate strategic options. The illustration is simple and provides an example of some of the basic analysis required before the more advanced principles can be applied: it is fictitious and is not intended to bear any resemblance to a real company or situation.

Background

A large UK-based composite insurance company, a household name selling personal and commercial insurance products, has suffered from a recent history of losses. The company wishes to investigate areas for future expansion in the personal insurance area. It particularly wants to understand the threat of new entrants.

The management team's mission and objective are: 'To become universally accepted as "the best".'

Their stated objective is to use their talents creatively to build an increasingly successful and profitable business that:

● gives the highest quality service to all customers
● focuses on areas that maximise profitability
● improves shareholder value.

An overview of the flow of business is given in Figure 35 below.

Figure 35 *Business flow*

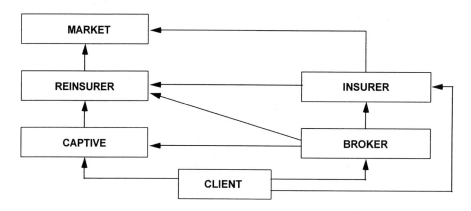

Spreading of risk through reinsurance will significantly affect the underwriting result to the insurer.

The overall programme of strategic analysis is given in Figure 36 below. This case study demonstrates the information required to develop and implement a strategy to explore new business opportunities.

Figure 36 *Programme for strategy formulation*

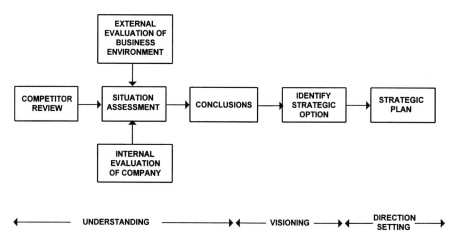

Industry and market

Starting with the external perspective, the key factors in the macro-environment are those listed in Table 10 below.

Table 10 *Relevant macro-environmental factors*

Political	Economic	Social	Technological
EC Third Directive opening up UK to foreign insurers	Terrorism	Demographics	IT systems
UK government influence on recovery, interest rates, tax regime	Crime rates	Changes in home ownership	Expert systems
Health/safety legislation	'Sue for everything' mentality	Interest rates	Communications
Company car legislation	Economic growth prospects	Catastrophes	

The table provides a broad overview within which the market and the company are placed. The first task is to understand the market. Basic, publicly available information shows that the market is growing (Figure 37) and that there is little change in the mix of business volume between personal and commercial business (Figure 38).

Figure 37 *Insurance market growth*

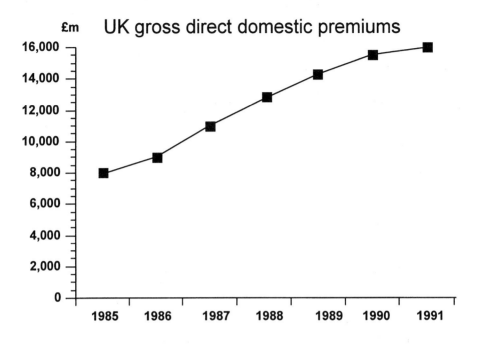

Figure 38 *General insurance market size*

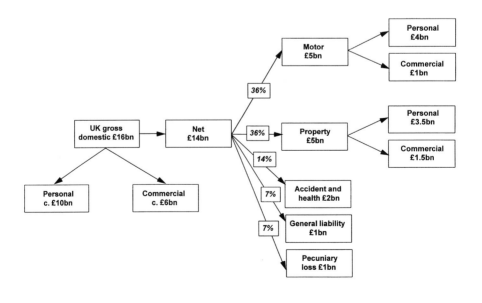

The next step is to 'drill down' into the key product groups to see if these are growing too. The key market drivers for insurance are based on the demand for the underlying assets that consumers purchase. Domestic insurance is driven by growth in households (Figure 39), penetration of consumer durables (Figure 40) and car ownership (Table 11). Again, from readily available published information the growth in demand can be found for the underlying assets.

Figure 39   *Growth in households*

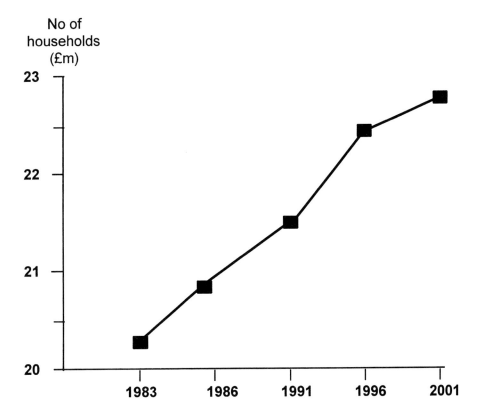

Figure 40   *Household penetration of consumer durables*

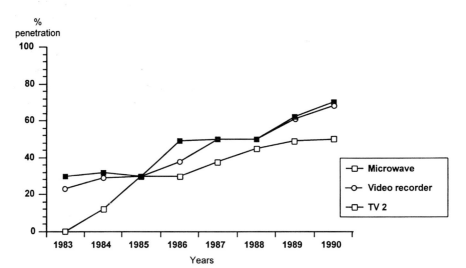

Table 11   *Car ownership (% households)*

	1981	*1991*
No car	39	33
One car only	45	44
Two or more cars	15	23
Cars per 1000 population	281	361

Car ownership will continue to rise.
Government taxing of car benefits may lead to switch between fleet and personal ownership.

What has yet to be determined is the current profitability of the insurance industry with regard to these markets. Figure 41 below shows that companies have experienced losses in the key fire and accident, and motor businesses.

Figure 41 *ABI – Fire and accident, and motor results*

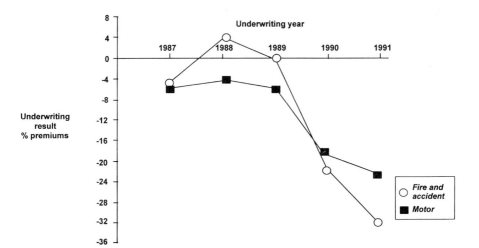

Companies have experienced losses across all lines of business.

In summary, there is growth in the underlying asset markets, the market is not profitable in any of these areas in total but there is probably untapped potential for those products where consumers have not taken insurance cover.

This overall analysis has still not revealed the nature of the forces at play in the industry and where there is profit to be made. To address this the structure of the industry must be examined in terms of the channels of distribution and the end-consumer's characteristics.

Supply chain and channels of distribution

Although in one sense the channel is an outlet for products, in another it is a rival for splitting the profit margin made from the final sale to the customer. The margin it can command depends on its relative power, which may vary by product. Table 12 (below) shows the products and agents dominating each product channel.

Table 12   *Industry forces: distribution channels*

Product	Purchase decision	Distribution power
Motor	Car	Brokers, auto associations, direct
House	House	Lenders, affinity groups
Contents	Home goods	Lenders, affinity groups, retailers
Travel	Holiday	Travel agents, leisure groups
Warranty	Home goods	Retailers

The channel mix varies considerably between products.

It is now necessary to have an understanding of the factors that are increasing or diminishing the power of the channel. These, as has been explained in the main body of this book, may be alliances, changes in territory or scope due to expansion or entry, and extensions of position based on current strengths.

Change in channel mix
- vertical integrations (insurers becoming distributors (sales companies, eg Direct Line))
- distributors forming close alliances with insurers (Automobile Association's links with specific panel of insurers)
- formation of retail chains by brokers (Swinton Insurance company)
- retailers selling warranty insurance on goods sold (forming captives).

The above lead to a blurring of the distinction between insurer and distributor.

Key trends
Of the key changes in the channels, the emergence of direct insurance appears to be the biggest threat. The direct distributors have the advantage of being able to set up a 'greenfield' site and therefore the potential to configure a low-cost, high-service process for dealing with the customer. Figure 42 below illustrates the downward-spiralling situation for traditional brokers and the virtuous circle created by the directs.

Figure 42 *Direct insurance channels benefit from a lower cost base*

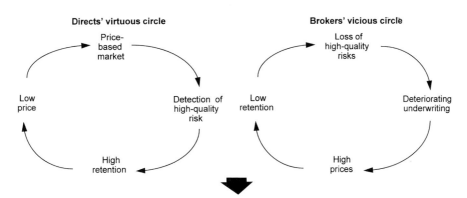

Polarisation of risks and channels –
in 1990–91 brokers lost 2% share to directs.

The bare rudiments of the position of Direct Line, the key player at the 'virtuous' end of the market, are sufficient to help understand what the benchmark for success is downstream from the insurance company.

Direct Line started 7 years ago. In 1991, its premiums increased by 90%. It insures 67,000 drivers (4.5% market share) and has made significant inroads into the home-insurance market (260,000 policies). Some of the factors that enabled the company to achieve this success were:

- centralised computer systems
- 18% expense ratio
- selective underwriting.

Despite the strong cost and focused nature of this type of competitor, it must be recognised that traditional brokers have an entrenched position and a major share of the distribution business. Their strengths are that they:

- make time to 'shop around' for the right policy for their client
- have some negotiating power with the underwriter
- help clients with settling their claims
- have relationships with loss adjusters.

The above illustrates that there is room to build differentiation and maintain a position in the face of cost-based competitors, perhaps by playing on the customer's need for assistance to secure settlement of claims.

Summary
At this stage, information has been gathered to help understand the industry, the market, the channels of distribution and the key trends. Next, the competitive forces need to be examined.

Competitive forces and position
Industry associations, market research and the knowledge of the company's management and front-line staff confirm that the main drivers of competition are as follows:

- industry growth in volume terms but premium growth likely to be limited
- significant overcapacity in the market
  - high fixed costs driving need for market share
  - leads to pressure on rates
- to the ultimate consumer there are little differences in products
  - any novel product will be quickly copied
- the use of intermediaries restricts the ability of brand awareness to generate sales
  - not the case with direct sales
- negligible switching costs.

In addition, there is a high degree of concentration of business volume in the hands of a few players.

These factors tend to intensify rivalry in the industry. Such high-level forces provide the basis upon which performance can be judged against rivals. The analysis in Table 13 below picks out the key factors from the customers' point of view and benchmarks them to the key rivals.

Table 13 *Competition*

	Client	A	B	C	Direct
Price	M	M	M	M	L
Branding	M	M	M	M	M
Product range	Wide	Wide	Wide	Wide	Targeted
Distribution	Multiple	Multiple	Multiple	Multiple	Single
Financial stability	M	M	M	M	M
Cost base	H	H	H	H	L
Competitive advantage	←——— Little differentiation ———→				H

H = High, M = Medium, L = Low

There is now enough information to make a stab at the basis of competition between the composite insurance business and its direct distributors. The reality of the misfortune of the composite's situation must be recognised and is summarised in Figure 43 below.

Figure 43 *Reality of current competitive position*

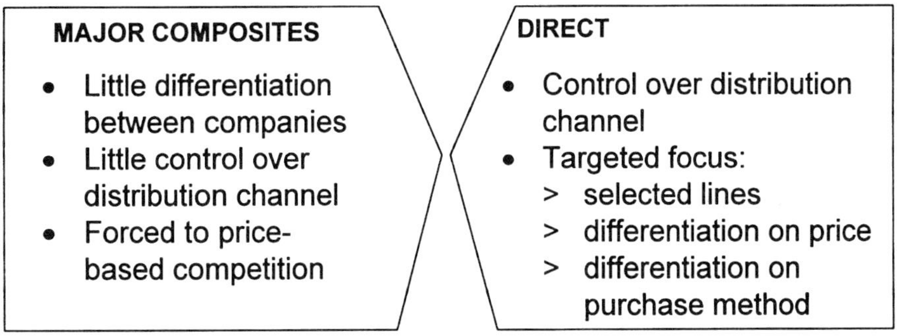

MAJOR COMPOSITES

- Little differentiation between companies
- Little control over distribution channel
- Forced to price-based competition

DIRECT

- Control over distribution channel
- Targeted focus:
  - > selected lines
  - > differentiation on price
  - > differentiation on purchase method

From information received, the following is known about the insurance industry:

- the market is expected to grow in volume terms but pressure on premium rates will continue
- existing composite competitors show little differentiation between themselves
  - most are in all areas
  - competition is based on price
  - volume-driven pricing strategies are adopted
- new entrants are a source of increasing threat because
  - they move from a base in motor to household insurance
  - customer-switching costs are low
  - cost structure enables competitive pricing to be adopted to build share
  - they have control over distribution channels

Options

Remembering the advice from Philip Kotler (see pp 101–111) on potential attack and defence strategies, there is a need to determine which options are available. Of relevance to this situation are the following:

(1) maintain the status quo (a position defence strategy)
(2) focus the business (this can be part of a guerrilla attack, an encirclement attack or a flanking attack)
(3) redefine the business (a bypass strategy)
(4) exit from the industry (a contraction defence or a withdrawal in recognition of defeat).

The external and internal information now need to be combined to help decide on strategy. The information regarding strengths and weaknesses is compiled through interviews, cost and profitability analysis, and asking customers their perceptions. The information-gathering, however, presents a dilemma – there are no obvious opportunities.

SWOT analysis

An assessment of capabilities is important to determine which options can be pursued by the company. A simple analysis of the strengths, weaknesses, opportunities and threats (SWOT) is presented in Figure 44 below.

Figure 44 *SWOT analysis*

Strengths	Weaknesses
❏ Brand name	❏ Lack of profitability
❏ Size	❏ Ability to differentiate against other competitors
❏ Distribution network	❏ Inability to understand product profitability
❏ Exposure spread over several segments	
Opportunities	**Threats**
?	❏ Success of direct insurers
	❏ Continued pressure – expansion of target market
	❏ Continued losses

Initial conclusions

Maintaining the status quo does not appear to be a viable medium- to longer-term strategy. A redefinition of the business and an exit strategy would ignore some of the key strengths of the business, for example its distribution network and size. The focusing of the business to overcome its weaknesses, such as lack of profitability and differentiation, would best help the company exploit its strengths in brand, distribution and size. Therefore, the basis of the focus strategy needs to be determined: the advantages and disadvantages of three of the key bases are given in Figure 45 below.

It is not within the scope of this book to present the detailed analysis necessary to evaluate these options, such as cost-benefit-risk analysis, projected cash-flows, capital requirements etc.

Figure 45   *Focus on different drivers of the business*

FOCUS

	Pros	Cons
By product line	☐ Reduce costs ☐ Improve returns	☐ High executions risk ☐ Higher concentration of risk
By distribution channel	☐ Closer relationships ☐ Channel education ☐ Reduce costs ☐ Long-term profitability	☐ Short-term losses ☐ Other channel reactions ☐ Possible decline in channel ☐ Competition reaction
Through new products	☐ Could build a niche ☐ Improve returns	☐ Easily copied ☐ Existing competition in niche ☐ Redeployment of development costs

Final conclusions

The summary information presented in this case study shows how information can be structured to proceed through a strategic evaluation process. The importance of information in strategy is clear – without it an organisation would not know its industry, market, competitive position, strengths, weaknesses and options. Such information is, today, fast becoming a commodity.

The second illustration is an example of how a company and its position can be assessed without any dialogue with the business itself.

ILLUSTRATION 2:
GATHERING RELEVANT INFORMATION WITHOUT ENTERING THE TARGET BUSINESS

This illustration provides an example of the data that can be collected from published sources in America and many European countries. The illustration is simple and provides an example of some of the basic analysis required before the more advanced principles can be applied. The illustration uses the names of real players in the UK DIY industry, but the new entrant is entirely fictitious. The choice of Wickes as a target is also entirely fictitious and the financial data has been altered, so that the 1996 concerns about trading practices at Wickes should not affect the validity of the case study. The tables and figures in this illustration contain fictional data of the type supplied by the Central Statistical Organisation, Business Monitor, Keynote, KPMG, ICC Financial Database, Verdict, statutory accounts, Datastream, the London Business School and the national and trade press.

Background
You are the chief executive officer of a major US public limited company in the slowly recovering US do-it-yourself market. Profits are squeezed with demand rising slowly as the economy stops and starts. Despite low interest rates and inflation and the fairly stagnant housing market, the uncertain employment scene prohibits a much-needed diversion of funds to home improvement.

You commission your strategy and planning unit to examine the options for you to enter the UK market – not because you believe it differs markedly in terms of prospects from the US but simply because you have pressure to grow, funds in the armoury and transferable management competencies.

This is the summary presentational report to you.

UK market drivers
The main factors driving the UK market are:

- the recession in the construction and DIY market persists
- there is greater competition in the DIY market due to the presence of 'sheds' as a result of
  - greater emphasis on display/merchandising
  - increased requirement to stock a broader product range
- cost control and increased operational efficiency are important to profitability resulting in
  - staff rationalisation
  - computerised stock control and EPOS
- the trend is to migrate to larger out-of-town sites and offer comprehensive services
- social trends indicate that although time spent on DIY as part of home-based leisure activities (see Table 14 below) has increased steadily since 1977, personal disposable income is static and loans for house purchases (a major factor affecting home improvements) have decreased
- the major share of the market for decorating and DIY supplies is held by the DIY retailers (see Table 15 below)
  - the trend is towards increased share of the market in the hands of these retailers.

Table 14 *Social trends 19Y3*

	19Z7	19X0	19X3	19X6	19X7	19Y0	19Y1
Home-based leisure activities % interviewees who participated in each activity during the 4 weeks prior to interview	52.5	55.5	54.0	52.5	64.5	64.5	
Personal disposable income (£bn at constant 1983 prices)				382.2	395.7	449.4	447.1
Loans for house purchase (£bn at constant prices)				40.5	44.1	48.9	40.2

Table 15 *Sale of decorators' DIY supplies by type of retail outlet (% value)*

	19Y0
DIY retailers	75.4
Mixed retailers	3.4
Hardware, china and fancy goods	2.9
General mail order	1.0
Other retailers	9.3
Carry-in	8.0
	100.0

All of the DIY retailers are owned by more powerful retail groups; the major stores are owned by high-performing high-street retailers (see Table 16 below).

Table 16 *Major DIY and decorating multiples*

	Owners	Number of stores	Turnover (£m)	Pre-tax profit (£m)	Advertising (£m)
B&Q	Kingfisher	420	1528.3	100.65	27.3
Texas	Ladbroke	336	97.95	38.1	33.9
Do It All	WH Smith and Boots	337.5	622.8	–5.1	17.7
Homebase	Sainsbury's	1.5	329.7	7.35	3.9
Wickes		100.5	278.7	25.65	3.75
Great Mills	RMC Group plc	130	280.5	13.95	3.6
AG Stanley	Boots	615	166.2	10.05	
Focus DIY	Focus Retail Group	42	69.45	3.3	

Annual accounts, 19Y2

19Y2 was characterised by the following:

- fierce price cuts
- an increase in the Do It All loss
- a price increase to customers for some products
- a freeze in prices paid to suppliers
- B&Q and Texas gave 20% blanket discounts
- Wickes gave a 4% discount off list prices
- Do It All followed with a 20% discount
- Homebase offered selective discounts.

In 19Y3 blanket discounts ended.

Industry structure – drivers of future performance

The power of the customer and the inherent intensity of rivalry due to the presence of long-standing and entrenched players make for a market that can be expected to spiral towards increased price and service competition. The industry structure analysis in Figure 46 and Table 17 below describes the key factors that will determine the profitability of the future players. An important point to note is that sufficient volume of business would reduce intensity of rivalry and that this is linked to the housing market and employment stability.

Figure 46   *Drivers of future performance*

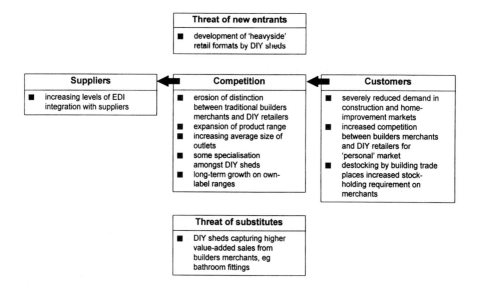

Table 17 *Forecast (19Y3): £bn at retail selling price*

	Core DIY products	Home improvements
19Y3	7.05	11.4
19Y4	7.3	11.7
19Y5	7.6	12.1
19Y6	7.6	12.3

UK supply chain

The supply chain of the industry is largely fragmented in terms of ownership, ie very few of the major players in the DIY markets are either vertically integrated forward into the building trade or backwards into manufacture. Wickes is the exception with a presence backstream in importing materials and upstream in property development (see Figure 47 below).

Figure 47 *UK supply chain (illustrative)*

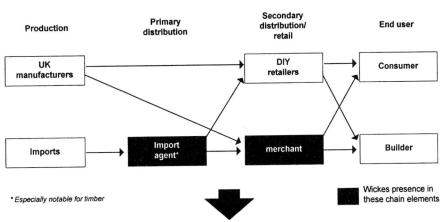

Wickes has integrated upstream into timber importing through the 1988 Hunter acquisition.

Trade formats

The two major formats are DIY sheds and builders merchants. Both of these have blurred their distinctions in an effort to attract a broader cross-section of customers (see Figure 48 below).

Figure 48 *Comparison of trade formats*

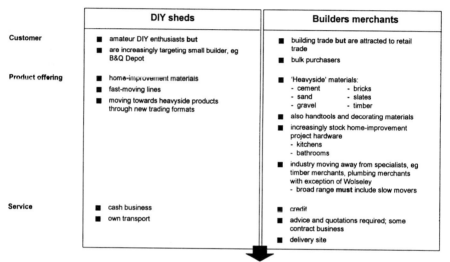

	DIY sheds	Builders merchants
Customer	■ amateur DIY enthusiasts **but** ■ are increasingly targeting small builder, eg B&Q Depot	■ building trade **but** are attracted to retail trade ■ bulk purchasers

Product offering	■ home-improvement materials
	■ fast-moving lines
	■ moving towards heavyside products through new trading formats
		■ 'Heavyside' materials:
		  - cement - bricks
		  - sand - slates
		  - gravel - timber
		■ also handtools and decorating materials
		■ increasingly stock home-improvement project hardware
		  - kitchens
		  - bathrooms
		■ industry moving away from specialists, eg timber merchants, plumbing merchants with exception of Wolseley
		  - broad range **must** include slow movers

Service	■ cash business ■ own transport	■ credit ■ advice and quotations required; some contract business ■ delivery site

Considerable blurring has occurred in the distinction between DIY sheds and the traditional builders merchants.

Competitive position

Information regarding the competitive position of the top six companies in each sector (see Figure 49 below) reveals that only Wickes has a position in both sectors. The DIY sector is dominated by companies owned by major high-street retailers.

The profitability-market share analysis of the major companies in Figure 50 below shows that Wickes is the least profitable with the lowest share and Texas the most. Market share growth appears to be correlated with profitability growth.

Figure 49   Competitive position

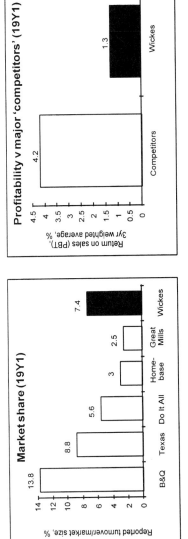

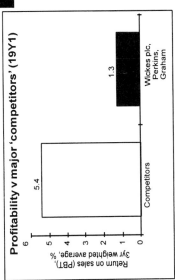

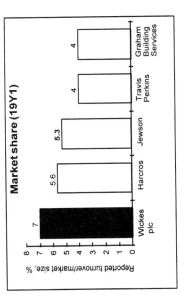

DIY sector

Builders merchants sector

Market share (19Y1)

Profitability v major 'competitors' (19Y1)

'Wickes makes up for rock bottom margins by generating sales per square foot miles ahead of its nearest rival'

(*Financial Times*, 27 July 1988)

Figure 50 *Competitive drivers*

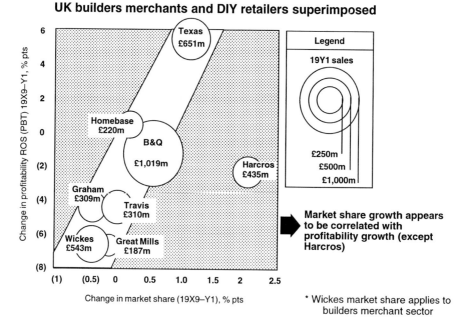

UK builders merchants and DIY retailers superimposed

Change in market share (19X9–Y1), % pts

* Wickes market share applies to builders merchant sector

Competitive position – operations comparison
The operations profile of the three key competitors (see Figure 51 below) shows some interesting differences:

- B&Q has the biggest stores, the greatest number of them and sells a broad range of products
- Texas is comparable in operation to B&Q but has a greater penetration of its own-label products
- Wickes approach differs markedly from the others with a lower number of stores, highest own-label penetration (97% of all lines are own-label) and the highest sales per square foot.

Figure 51 *Operations profile*

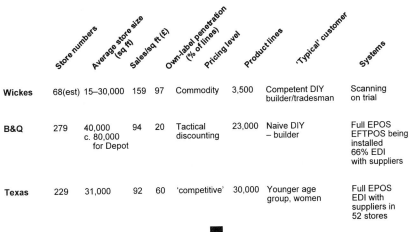

	Store numbers	Average store size (sq ft)	Sales/sq ft (£)	Own-label penetration (% of lines)	Pricing level	Product lines	'Typical' customer	Systems
Wickes	68(est)	15–30,000	159	97	Commodity	3,500	Competent DIY builder/tradesman	Scanning on trial
B&Q	279	40,000 c. 80,000 for Depot	94	20	Tactical discounting	23,000	Naive DIY – builder	Full EPOS EFTPOS being installed 66% EDI with suppliers
Texas	229	31,000	92	60	'competitive'	30,000	Younger age group, women	Full EPOS EDI with suppliers in 52 stores

Wickes approach differs from the leading DIY sheds and achieves greater sales density from a narrower (own-label) product range in, typically, smaller stores.

Regional analysis

The UK regional analysis in Figure 52 below demonstrates that the major players, B&Q and Texas, have a presence in every region. Do It All also has good UK coverage with a strong emphasis on the North West and Wales. Wickes has little presence in Scotland, Wales and the North.

Targeting

The information obtained so far suggests:

- a low-profit market with stable if not stagnant future returns until the UK property market takes off – this would provide volume to boost the DIY sector
- a number of diverse rivals across two sectors, each cross-trading to secure a wider customer base
- a number of geographically well-spread players, with some smaller players focusing on a few regions
- costs and service rather than cost or service will characterise the future.

Figure 52 *UK regional analysis: retail operations (19Y1)*

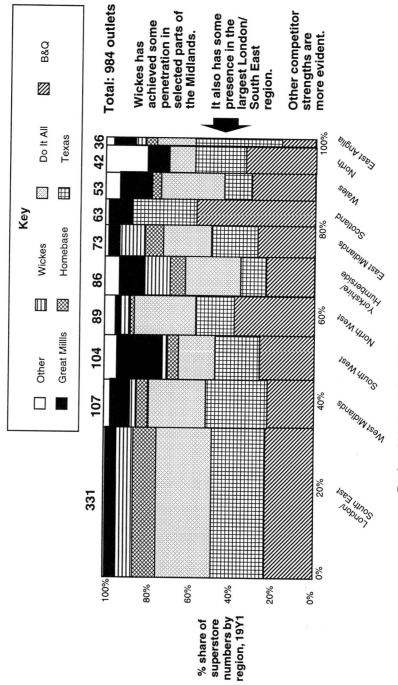

Figure 53 *Strategic options*

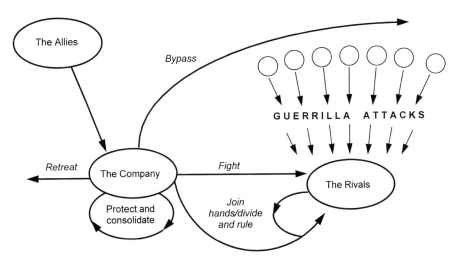

The options (illustrated in Figure 53 above) are to:

(1) reject this market until and if it becomes more attractive
(2) take a position in this market, perhaps a joint venture or other alliance, in anticipation of a rise in market volume
(3) enter aggressively now and establish a position.

According to the strategy and planning unit the balance of evidence indicates that option 2 should be the preferred choice. Given such a strategy they recommend that Wickes be examined as a candidate (see note at the beginning of this case study).

Financial analysis
The financial results of the company are poor (see Figures 54–58 below). The company appears to have grown rapidly until 19X9 in terms of turnover, profitability and returns. Thereafter its results have dropped away. Productivity has dropped from 19X7; almost halving to the period to date.

Figure 54   *Group turnover*

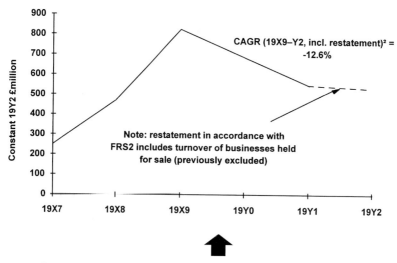

Wickes' sales have declined steadily since 19X9, reflecting recession in the construction
and home-improvement sectors.

Figure 55   *Return on sales (PBT*)*

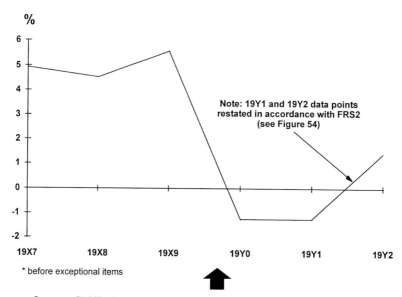

Group profitability has been hit hard by reduced customer demand and increased competition.
The improvement in 19Y2 reflects debt reduction and cost control in the timber businesses.

Figure 56 *Group return on capital employed (PBT*)*

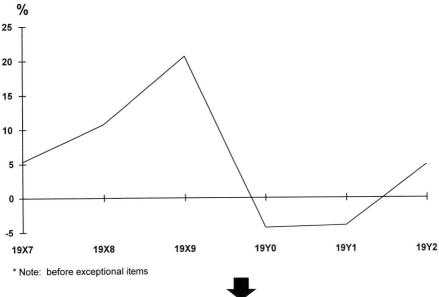

* Note: before exceptional items

Return on capital has been erratic.

Figure 57 *Gearing*

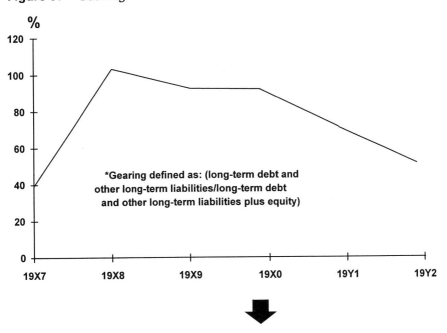

The group has progressively reduced debt since the Hunter Timber acquisition.

Figure 58   *Employee productivity*

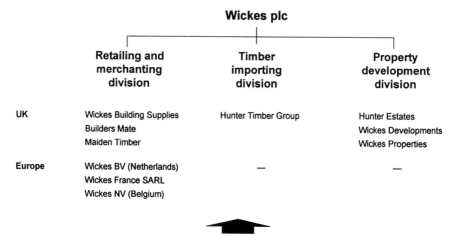

Employee productivity rose slightly in 19Y2 following cost control.
This arrested the previous four years of decline.

Figure 59   *Organisation structure and principal subsidiaries*

Wickes plc

	Retailing and merchanting division	Timber importing division	Property development division
UK	Wickes Building Supplies Builders Mate Maiden Timber	Hunter Timber Group	Hunter Estates Wickes Developments Wickes Properties
Europe	Wickes BV (Netherlands) Wickes France SARL Wickes NV (Belgium)	—	—

The group is organised on a business segment basis. Retailing and merchanting is the main customer for
the timber-importing division.

Organisation

The group is organised on a business segment basis with a substantial amount of internal trading between divisions – retailing and merchanting is a major customer for the timber-importing division (see Figure 59 above).

Divisional performance

Divisional financial analysis shows the timber-importing and distributing business to be dragging group profitability down (see Figures 60 and 61 below). At this stage, it is unclear whether this is because of cross-subsidisation between division, or inequitable transfer charges or actual poor performance in that business.

Figure 60 *Divisional split*

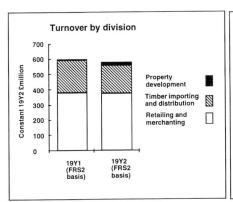
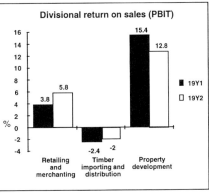

The core retailing and merchanting division has increased profitability.
The declining timber importing business has remained loss-making.

Figure 61 *Divisional analysis*

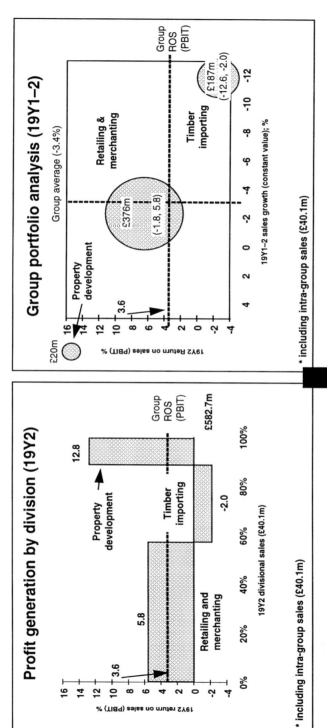

Profit generation by division (19Y2)

Group portfolio analysis (19Y1–2)

Retailing and merchanting is the group's profit 'engine'.

Importing appears to be poorly positioned but provides 'flow-through' benefits to the retailing operations.

Figure 62 *International geographic split*

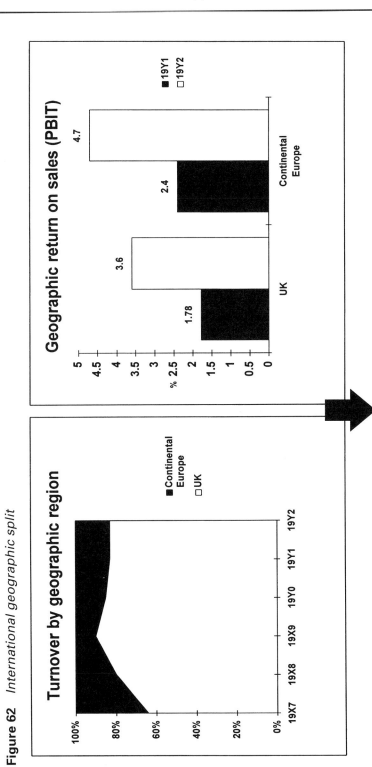

Figure 62 *International geographic split*

The UK dominates the group's activities although Continental business is more profitable.

International coverage

The UK dominates the business representing about 80% of turnover but yielding less in return on sales than continental Europe (see Figure 62 above).

Share price movement

Over the last year the share price has bounced back and brokers, on the whole, expect a comeback in performance. The 5-year trend shows Wickes to have been consistently outperformed by the FT All-Share and the FT Building Materials share indices (see Figure 63 below).

Evident strategy

Determining what the evident strategy of an organisation may be is an art rather than a science. It requires you to put yourself in the shoes of management and fathom their response to the situation.

From what has been seen of the UK market, Wickes' evident strategy has three key features (see Figure 64 below):

- focusing on the trade customer rather than the average householder – but failing to serve either superbly well
- extensive promotion of own-label but failing to satisfy the middle-class, *Which?* magazine reader who is willing to pay more for branded products such as Wickes
- growth by acquisition (see Figure 65 below) – it is uncertain how successful the integration of these companies is and whether the management, systems and cultural implications have been adequately addressed.

Figure 63 *Shareprice movement*

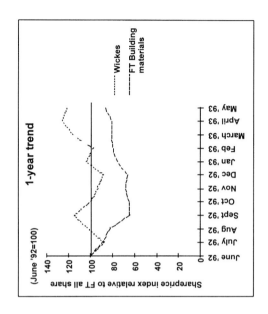

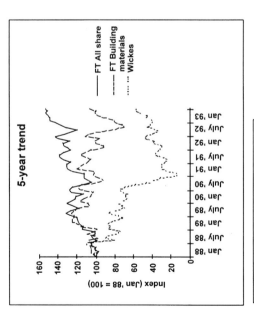

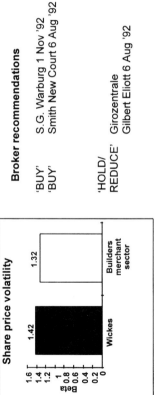

Broker recommendations

'BUY' S.G. Warburg 1 Nov '92
'BUY' Smith New Court 6 Aug '92

'HOLD/
REDUCE' Girozentrale
Gilbert Eliott 6 Aug '92

Broker comments

'shareholders should be reassured by the encouraging progress recorded by the original DIY interests'
(S.G. Warburg 1 Nov '92)

'in the absence of any signs of general recovery in Wickes timber markets we believe the shares are likely to continue to drift' (Girozentrale Gilbert Eliott 6 Aug '92)

Figure 64   *Evident strategy*

Differentiation	– focused at heavy end of DIY sector
	– focused product range of 3,500 lines (cf 20–30,000 typical in DIY)
	– targeted at competent DIY enthusiast/tradesmen
	– new retail formats being rolled out
	– Builders Mate (commodity builders merchants)
	– focus on hardware needed for improvement projects
Product development	– home-improvement projects
	– 30% of floorspace to be rolled out to 75% of stores by December 1993
	– quality timber
	– lighting, door-fittings, handtools
	– intends to reduce dependence on trade customer base
Own-label range development	– 97% of product lines
	– commodity own label and own branding
Supply chain integration	– Timber importing (Hunter) into timber and building materials retailing (Wickes/Maiden)
Supplier partnerships	– pan-European purchasing from 22 suppliers
Retail network expansion	– 11 new UK openings in 19Y2, up to 14 planned in 19Y3
	– UK target of 200 stores (target date not specified)
Selective international retail expansion	– France, Belgium and Netherlands

Wickes has pursued a niche strategy in UK retailing complemented by supply-chain integration and selective UK and Continental expansion.

Figure 65   *Corporate activity 1988–1993*

	Date	Name/type	Value	Comments
Acquisitions	Sept '88	Hunter plc	£283m	Acquired from Hillsdown Holdings
Disposals	July '90	Parker Kilsingbury	c. £4.5m total	MBO of Hunter subsidiary
	Sept '89	Mallinsons of Swords	Undisclosed	Eire subsidiary
	July '89	Fitchett & Woolacott	£6m	
		Whitmore Timber	£2.8m	MBO of Hunter subsidiaries
	Nov '88	Allan Bros		
		Adamson Joinery	£4.3m	MBO of Hunter subsidiaries
	Nov '88	Hunter Plywood (Bristol)	£2.1m	
		Kesma/Midland Joinery	£1.9m	MBO of Hunter subsidiaries
Financings	Feb '91	Rights issue	£42.6m	99.4% taken
	Nov '88	Multiple credit facility	£150m	Process to finance purchase of Hunter plc
	March '88	Rights issue	£28.7m	To eliminate debt raised by 1987 MBO of Wickes from US parent

The group has undertaken a number of disposals following the 1988 Hunter Timber acquisition and reduced debt through its successful 1991 rights issue.

SWOT analysis

The strengths, weaknesses, opportunities and threats (SWOT) analysis in Figure 66 below shows that the opportunities for Wickes, given its strengths, outweigh the threats. It has some surmountable weaknesses that investment could help overcome.

Figure 66 *SWOT analysis*

Strengths	Weaknesses
■ leading position in builders merchant segment ■ trade customer base ■ own-label branding ■ independence	■ market share underperformance v competitors ■ patchy UK regional coverage ■ not as profitable as other builders merchants ■ lack of major parentage
Opportunities	**Threats**
■ reduce gearing further ■ increase employee productivity further ■ continued European expansion in retail ■ improve merchandising to compete favourably with DIY sheds ■ improve information systems ■ verify own market positioning through retail site portfolio analysis and customer research	■ continued loss of market share to DIY sheds 　– heavyside 　– added-value 'consumer' products ■ reliance on UK construction sector may protract profit underperformance

The proposal for adding value to Wickes

Issue	*Proposal outline*
low profitability	• introduce cost reduction programmes of the type that has been successful in the US business • optimise store portfolio to transfer best practice across stores and ensure only the profitable or strategic are retained • integrate processes and systems better between importing and retailing to gain economies

Issue	*Proposal outline*
poor information technology relative to competitors	• implement bespoke US retailing systems with minor modifications for the UK
poor staff productivity	• introduce better processes, training and skilled resources
gearing remains high	• increase equity
opportunity harvest	• **outline proposal**
resolve the 'stuck in middle' position	• create a consumer-focused new concept Wickes format and introduce Wickes as a store within a store
merchandising is key to capturing the unsophisticated buyer	• apply high-street retail skills which have been so successful in US
attractive regions remain uncovered	• invest to enter attractive regions
further decrease buying costs	• combine forces to exercise greater buying power.

Conclusion

The summary information presented in this case study shows how readily available information is to carry out initial evaluations of strategic options. Without ever entering a company, information can be accessed on many of its key strengths and weaknesses relative to its main competitors. This information can then be used to determine strategy.

BIBLIOGRAPHY

BOOKS

Dornbusch and Fischer *Macroeconomics* (McGraw-Hill, 1981)

Elting, John R. *The Superstrategists* (WH Allen, 1987)

Hamel and Prahalad *Competing for the Future* (Harvard Business School Press, 1994)

Handy, Charles *Understanding Organisations* (Penguin Books, 1986)

The Age of Unreason (Business Books Ltd, 1989)

Kaplan, Robert S. and Thomas Johnson, H. *Relevance Lost* (Harper & Row, 1987)

Kotler, Philip *Marketing Management: Analysis, Planning, Implementation and Control* (Prentice Hall, 8th edn, 1994)

Porter, Michael E. *Competitive Strategy: Techniques for Analyzing Industries and Competitors* (The Free Press, 1980)

Tzu, Sun *The Art of War* ed James Clavell (Hodder & Stoughton, 1981)

ARTICLES

Bowen, David 'Double agent in the office' *Independent on Sunday*, 17 October 1993

Hamel, Prahalad and Doz 'Collaborate with your competitors' *Harvard Business Review*, November 1989

Hampden-Turner, C. 'Getting wiser about the Asians' *Director*, June 1994

Kaplan, Robert S. and Norton, D. 'The Balanced Scorecard – measures that drive performance' *Harvard Business Review*, January–February 1992

Oliff, M. and Collies, R. 'GE's brave new world' *Business Week*, 8 November 1993

'Expert systems – the bridge to intelligent manufacturing' *Imede Perspective for Managers*, no 5, 1989

Pagons, William G. 'The work of the leader' *Harvard Business Review*, November–December 1992

Smart, T. 'Can Xerox duplicate its glory days?' *Business Week*, 4 October 1993

Thierrien, L. and Hoots, C. 'Café au lait, a croissant and trix' *Business Week*, 24 August 1992

Verity, J.W. 'Taking a laptop on a call' *Business Week*, 25 October 1993

COMPANY INDEX

References are to page numbers.

SUBJECT INDEX

References are to page numbers.